Coven of the Catta

Elders and History
Unique Ritual Practices
And Spells

Written and Compiled by
Gary Lee Hoke

ISBN # 978-0-557-95344-8
Pages 137

Quotes – Some are from the Harvard Yearbook 25th anniversary of the class of 1924. The quoted notes from the master's thesis are from a document I found in the library, author unnamed.

Photo credits – Many are by the author. Some were given to me by Lady Phoebe. Others are listed with their credits or with no credits where I have not been able to trace the photographer.

Acknowledgements - I would first like to thank Tabatha Ferrell for lighting a fire under my butt to get me to finally write this book after it sat as rough notes for years. Thanks to Adonis Merlin for help with proofreading and photo editing. And thanks to Tony Oliveri for showing me how to edit this in Word for the publisher and for his encouragement.

Author's Note – the first part of this book was originally published separately at Lulu.com as *A History of Dr Frederick LaMotte Santee and the Coven of the* Catta © 2010 ISBN#978-0-557-85997-9.

This author takes full responsibility for any mistakes made in the writing of this book.

Table of Contents

Part I – A History of Dr. Frederick LaMotte Santee and the Coven of the Catta

Part II – Coven of the Catta Unique Ritual Practices and Spells

Part I – A History of Dr. Frederick LaMotte Santee and the Coven of the Catta

Introduction

On this All Hallows Samhain 31 October 2010, now almost 30 years after the death of Dr. Frederick LaMotte Santee and the beginning of my involvement in the Coven of the Catta of Wapwallopen Pennsylvania and beyond, I am writing what I know of this history.

Contact with the Coven of the Catta

We arrived at the book house of the late Dr. Santee's in 1981. My witch girlfriend and I had seen an ad in Circle Network News about a coven located in Wapwallopen, about 100 miles northeast of where we resided outside of Harrisburg Pennsylvania. We arrived and were led into his 50,000 volume book house where we were greeted by three elder ladies, Janee the High Priestess, Jeannie and Judy sitting in rocking chairs around a roaring fireplace flanked by large iron cauldrons. It couldn't be more archetypal "witchy". They denied having placed that ad and were amazed at our arrival.

Santee Bookhouse Fireplace © GLHoke

We arrived there one year after Dr. Santee's death and everything was in disarray. The temple was full of items salvaged from Santee's house and the book house had suffered a fire that year which left a hole in the roof. We asked for teaching and initiation and Janee aka Edna Jane Kishbaugh-Williams aka Lady Phoebe Athene Nimue (acronym Lady PAN) accepted us. Their mood was somber as they had lost the center of their coven, Dr Frederick LaMotte Santee aka Lord Merlin, their High Priest. I will speak much more on him later.

Biography of Lady Phoebe

Here is a short biographical note on Lady Phoebe. She was an amazing lady. Phoebe or Janee was the High Priestess of the remaining coven members and is the witch who taught and initiated me. She was born in Berwick Pennsylvania on 13 April 1921. She met Dr. Santee in 1956 and was his receptionist-secretary at the Santee Medical office and Santee Memorial Library in Wapwallopen, Pa. They both had married partners but they were each other's platonic soul mates. She had no children. She was afflicted with a degenerative arthritic disease which left her body twisted, one leg shorter than the other and her nose was replaced with an artificial one. Of course like all of Santee's girls she wore high heels even in her condition.

I obtained a lot of old photos from 1965 of Santee's girls and they were all in high heels, skirts just above the knee, faux fur coats and cat's eye glasses. Phoebe was an artist from a young age and she actually met Lady Alsace or Jeannie at a painting class. She drew a lot of the illustrations and wrote poetry and invocations for the Coven. Here is one of her drawings, and in the Addendum there are poems listed.

She wrote a column in the local newspaper called "The Witches Kettle". She also wrote and edited the Coven's publication entitled "The Cat's Tale". In 1967 she and Dr. Santee were initiated by Sybil Leek. Phoebe has said that she remembers previous lives, one of which was the wife of an Indian chief who lived along the Susquehanna river hundreds of years ago. She was a strong wiled Aires and we did not always agree on everything, but she was my mentor who taught me how to be a witch and a Priest.

She passed away on 5 December 2005 at the age of 84 and is buried in the Pine Grove Cemetery in Berwick, Pa. When I went to visit her grave a few years ago there was a small box built in front of it with rocks and flowers inside. On the edge of the box it said *I am watching* with some crescent moons around, almost warning people to not vandalize the site. I lit a red candle in remembrance but know she is not there. About a year ago I had a vivid dream that I was flying in a stormy night and to the left of me was Santee and Phoebe flying on brooms and they were both just staring intensely at me. So I know she is with her soul mate flying around and having a good ole witch time.

Lady Phoebe circa 1965

Courtesy Dave Hoag

Lady Triumphant from the Cat's Tale

Lady Phoebe Athene Nimue circa 1985
Edna Jane Kishbaugh Williams © GLHoke

Edna Kishbaugh Williams

Former aide to doctor enjoyed drawing

Edna Kishbaugh Williams, 84, formerly of 531 E. Fourth St., Nescopeck, died 12:03 p.m. Monday, Dec. 5, 2005, in Berwick Retirement Village II.

Edna was born in Berwick, April 13, 1921, a daughter of the late Edgar and Mary Slusser Kishbaugh.

She attended the former Nescopeck High School.

She retired as a receptionist-secretary with the late Dr. Frederick L. Santee, Wapwallopen, after his death in 1980.

She enjoyed drawing.

She was preceded in death by her husband, Dale Williams, on Feb. 22, 1998, and by two brothers: Ethan and Ralph Kishbaugh.

She will be remembered by nieces and nephews and their families.

Private services will be held with the Rev. Rodney Miller, pastor of Wesley United Methodist Church, Nescopeck, officiating. She will be laid to rest next to her beloved husband in Pine Grove Cemetery, Walnut Street, Berwick.

Obituary of Edna Jane Kishbaugh Williams

Grave of

Edna Jane Kishbaugh Williams © GLHoke

History of the Coven of the Catta

The Coven of the Catta was formed around 1967 by Santee and Phoebe as I shall call them from here on. They both loved cats and supported the Humane Society and gave the coven the totem of the cat "Bastet" from Egypt. Santee had been familiar with many in the occult world including Sybil Leek. They met in NYC and she was invited to Wapwallopen. When Sybil arrived at the covenstead, according to Phoebe, she and the doctor's secretary-librarians asked her to teach and initiate them into witchcraft to form a coven. Sybil's lineage was from the Coven of the Horsa from the New Forest area SE of London England. She also hung out with and learned a lot from the Gypsies and their magickal ways. Before that the lineage came from Coven of the Red Dragon in Gorge de Loup (Wolf Gorge) in SE France. Santee himself, as I shall expand on later, carried a handful of witchcraft and occult lineages from Europe. The combination became the Coven of the Catta. At first they had their temple in the cellar of Santee's house.

Santee House Cellar Temple 1970

Sometime in the 1970s Dr. Santee had a cinder block building built right next to his house and doctor's office. Over the years he amassed a library that contained 50,000 books on all manner of subjects, from the Greek and Latin classics he loved to history and religion, including a fairly large occult section. There was the main room with fireplace and his large desk, another room with a round table for classes, a strong vault for the really old tomes dating back to the 17th century, and in the back a room used for rituals. After the bookhouse was built, they moved their temple from the old to the new one in full ceremonial garb. From 1967 to 1980, the year of Santee's death, the coven flourished with mostly members from the local community. In fact the Coven and the Doctor are somewhat of an urban legend in the area now with rumors of Satanism and cat sacrifices! The fact is they were just practicing good ole white witchcraft from everything I can see. They also published a newsletter called "The Cat's Tale" in which various articles, spells and pictures were submitted by the main coven members. These articles were written with a typewriter back then and mimeographed for circulation. I wrote articles for this newsletter on my 1987 era Mac computer, which at the time was oh so high tech. This just reminds me how far we have come, from having to write letters on paper and mail them to people to nowadays where witches communicate through their email, blogs, social media sites and websites.

In 1979 someone broke into the bookhouse to steal some of the doctor's 16th century books and gold and silver bars, then set fire to the place to cover it up. The resident cat Bastet was killed in the fire but left this mark. The place never fully repaired and the doctor died the next year.

$500,000 fire loss

This interior photograph of a portion of "The Book House" of Dr. Frederick Santee, Wapwallopen physician, shows some of the thousands of volumes that were burned or ruined by fire Tuesday evening. Although insured for $300,000, the area doctor estimated the loss at in excess of $500,000. Many of the books, collected for more than 50 years, were rare Greek and Latin volumes. Some of the books dated back to the 17th century. A state police fire marshal indicated the blaze may have been caused by a defective electric plug on a coffee machine. An investigation into the fire is continuing. The 71-year-old physician said, "It's like seeing a lifetime fall in and crash around you," as he looked over the debris. (Staff Photo)

Wapwallopen fire destroys valuable book collection

A Tuesday evening fire at a building adjacent to the home of Dr. Frederick Santee, Wapwallopen, destroyed or seriously damaged thousands of volumes of rare and valuable books.

A three-section, concrete block structure constructed by the Wapwallopen physician was known as "The Book House." Reports indicated that fire of undetermined origin began in an annex near the rear of the main library building. The fire was centered near a furnace and refrigerator, it was said.

Flames were discovered at about 6 p.m. Tuesday and by the time firemen arrived at the scene the fire had eaten through the ceiling and portions of the roof.

It was indicated that approximately 500,000 volumes were stored in the Santee private library. Many were first edition publications while others were rare Greek and Latin writings.

The collection of books had been the work of the 71-year-old physician and was widely known and used as a research center for scholars throughout the eastern United States.

Dr. Santee is the third generation of his family to practice medicine in the community of Wapwallopen.

A state police fire marshal has been called in to assist in the probe of the blaze.

No damage estimate was available at press time Wednesday.

7-5-9

Local article about the bookhouse fire

Outline of Bastet Cat © GLHoke

And that brings us up to 1981 when my Priestess Lady Iska Nuit Aradia and I arrived. Over the next few months we drove almost a hundred miles north, cleaned out the temple, re-painted the three circles as prescribed, and rituals began again with some people from that area and mostly witches who came up from the Harrisburg area 8 times a year for Sabats. I drove up even more often to hand copy my own three "Books of Shadows" from Lady Phoebe's two books, which is over 300 pages of material. Unfortunately when she passed all her possessions, including these books, were just thrown into the dumpster. Most of the material is from the books on witchcraft available in the 1970s, and the rituals mostly from Lady Sheba's Books of Shadows. What Phoebe taught was what is called today "Old Guard Wicca". We were taught to do the rituals as they were written in the books with no additions or subtractions. I suppose it is similar to a Catholic doing the Mass over and over. It may sound boring but there is a certain comfort in this type of ritual. The rituals for the Sabats were almost exactly alike except for short lines and ritual actions that were specific to the season. When it was time for our third degree initiation in which we were supposed to write our own ritual, Phoebe was not pleased with what we put together because it was too far off the original rituals. Away from the Sabats we would often drive up and take Phoebe out into the woods at special places she loved. We would go up on Council Cup the nearby mountain and in the picture above she taught us how to call the winds by whistling for them. She felt close to her AmerIndian past life and would tell us stories about it. At one place where her father had helped build an old stone bridge, out in the woods, she showed us the white spirit snake that Sybil had passed on to her, and that spirit was passed on to me at my first degree and integrated into my magicke. One thing about the COC system is that there is a lot of physical work between Probationership and the First degree and it does take a year and a day. In fact, that time period is between all the degrees. There are instruments to be made and found and consecrated. You can't just buy everything on the internet like nowadays. We got blisters and bleeding fingers cutting our wands and besoms. For 9 years (1981-1990) we led a coven of many members who came and went. We and a handful of other witches were initiated into our higher degrees over time. I will detail these initiations at the end of this article.

HPT Shawnus Merlin Belarion

Covenstead Temple 1980s

My Priestess and I eventually parted ways. Due to witch politics I eventually withdrew from being High Priest of the Coven and let things wane down, as they did. I had my fallings out with Lady Phoebe at times, but eventually was also reconciled with her a few years before her death. Phoebe lost possession of the doctor's house and bookhouse and the latter fell into a more dilapidated state. I started doing the rituals again in her presence with Lady Alsace Isa Brie, an early elder member of the coven, as my Priestess. She is an Australian, a gifted psychic and wonderful gardener. We do these rituals mostly outside a couple times a year on her hilltop property outside Berwick, Pa. Sadly Lady Phoebe passed in 2005 and now the celebrants who come are mostly witches from other lineages and pagan friends.

High Priestess Lady Alsace Isa Brie

I also started having Lady Alsace down to my place north of Harrisburg to celebrate Sabats, usually at All Hallows. I have a temple set up on the first floor and in the cellar for larger groups. Witches from other lineages are freely invited and do come to these rituals.

HPT Shawnus Merlin Belarion 2003

Shawnus Cellar Temple 2010

A Biography of Dr. Frederick LaMotte Santee

At his point I will write all I know about Dr. Santee, which is from Phoebe's stories, some articles I found in the Santee Memorial Library and from the Harvard Yearbooks. I never met him, having arrived one year after his passing, but he was an amazing man, doctor, scholar and occultist.

He was born 17 September 1906 in Wapwallopen, Pa. He was born in a lineage of four generations of doctor's who practiced medicine. His grandfather was a Civil War surgeon who helped runaway slaves. His father was Charles LaMotte Santee who held MD degrees from LaFayette and Jefferson colleges in 1901 and he passed away in 1963. His mother was Verna Caroline Lloyd Santee.

Santee showed signs of genius at an early age. By age 3 he would read both English and German. He learned Latin from his grandfather's grammar books. By age 8 he was translating Caesar's Gallic Wars from Latin into English and back again to check his grammar. He went to Wapwallopen High School and then on to Wilkes-Barre High School for his last year. He went to Central High School in Philadelphia for AB degree in Greek and had the highest score in the USA, and so went to Harvard.

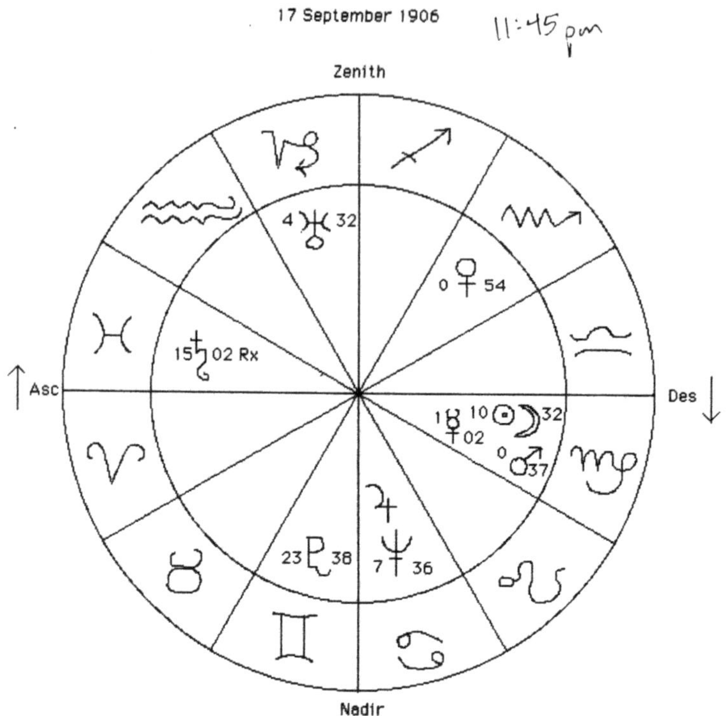

Santee Astrology

At age 14 he was the youngest person to attend Harvard from 1924-26 where he graduated at age 16 with an AB Magna Cum Laude.

At Harvard he met EK Rand, the Latin scholar with whom he corresponded for years. When asked "Who interested you in the occult?", he cites Harvard teacher Professor Grandient who taught Medieval literature and old French, George L. Kitridge who taught English and TM Boura.

He went to the University of Oxford England where he graduated age 18 in 1928 with an AB and then his MA in 1929. While at Oxford he jointed The Alpha et Omega Lodge of the Hermetic Order of the Golden Dawn where he met Aleister Crowley, HP Blavatsky, WB Yeats, Thomas Agee, Dion Fortune, AE Waite, and Israel Regarde. He also jointed Theosophical Society of England. At Oxford his main occult influence was from his philosophy teacher, a Professor Brabbart.

One source says he attended the University of Berlin in 1924-28 where he received his Ph.D. but this date does not seem to match the other records. He spent additional years in Rome, teaching positions at Harvard, Temple, Kenyon. Johns Hopkins, but held no tenure due to his socialist ideas. He was one of the 100 members of the Institute of Arts and Letters.

While at the University of Berlin he was initiated into witchcraft at a Coven 30 miles outside Berlin, the coven High Priest being an Arnold Reinman(d). In travels in the Middle East he met native adepts of the High Art in Egypt, learned from a German adept also in Egypt, and from a Sheik who was High Priest of a "coven" in North Africa.

Harvard's Three Time Honor Winner

FREDERICK L. SANTEE

SANTEE LEADS SENIOR CLASS

Youngest Member of Harvard '24 Hails from Pennsylvania

Santee youth

Santee as a young man

Santee claims to have been a Homeopathic Doctor to Adolf Hitler but escaped Germany before the War. Santee also claims to have adopted into the USA the daughter of Hitler, named Tao, whom Hitler fathered to an English lady before the War.

In 1928 he married Edith Rundle from Allentown, Pa. In 1930 they either birthed or adopted a daughter names Ruth who died in 1938.

In 1930 he was a Sheldon Fellow and Fellow at the American Academy of Rome for 3 years. By then he could read Latin, Greek, German and some Sanskrit.

In the later 1930s he spent 6 years teaching in the USA at Lehigh, Vanderbilt, Harvard, Temple, and Kenyon colleges. As noted before he never achieved tenure at any of these institutions. During this time he jointed the America Rosicrucian Society and was initiated into the Illuminati degree.

In 1938 he graduated from John's Hopkins University in Baltimore Maryland with his MD degree.

From 1938-1942? he taught classical languages at Kenyon College in Ohio USA and was involved in the Humanistic Revival (see issues of the Kenyon Review). He opposed the US entrance into WWII since he was an avowed Socialist.

Also in 1942 he divorced Edith Rundle and married Betty Addis of Cumberland, Md. They adopted Tao. Betty died in 1966.

From 1943-45 he was drafted into the Navy, served in the South Pacific, but saw no action. Later stationed in Arkansas USA he was a Lieutenant in the Medical Corps. Also at that time he published "Sawdust and Tomatoes" (poems of his and his mothers).

The Harvard Yearbook of 1957 lists him as living in Baltimore practicing medicine there. From letters it appears he knew John Colhane the Irish writer, David McDowell at Kenyon and Random House, Father Flye from NYC, Clyde Pharr, and other famous classicists.

In 1956 Santee met Edna Jane Kishbaugh Williams aka Lady Phoebe Athene Nimue.

In 1963 on his father's death, he returns to Wapwallopen Pennsylvania to continue his medical practice. His home and office were the same at 5 River Street.

In the 1970s once the library was built next door he employed a total of 2 nurses and 4 secretaries and librarians. He wrote a newspaper column called: "The Country Doctor" and Janee wrote a column called: "The Witches' Kettle". The locals says he was a kind and compassionate doctor, though a bit of an eccentric. He often treated the poor at no charge.

Santee aged 43

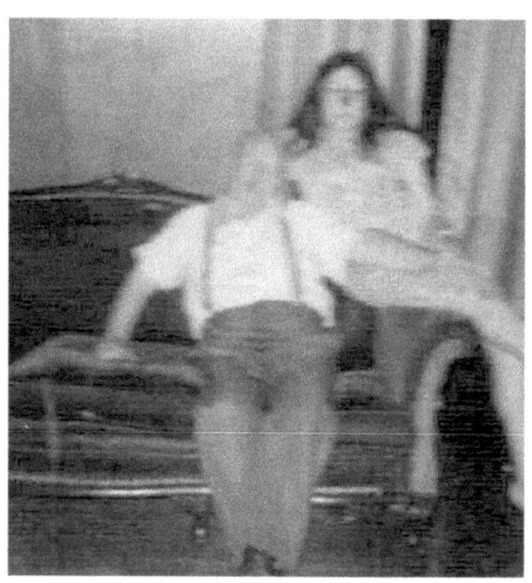

Santee and Phoebe - Soul Mates

Santee house/office

Santee Bookhouse

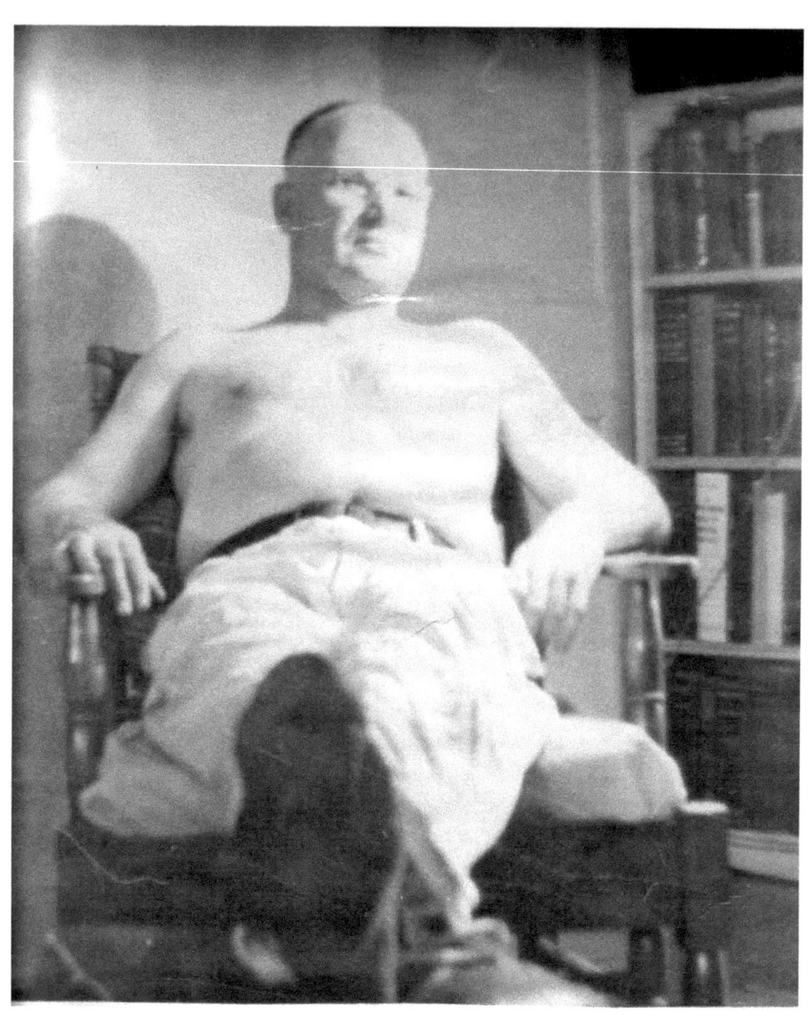

Herr Doktor

***The Devil's Wager* book cover**
Exposition Press

Santee was known to have rubbed shoulders with much of the northeastern occult community. He was also a scholar of the Faust novels and legend and wrote his own Faustian story entitled "The Devil's Wager" set in modern times. He had a leg and nylon fetish if I can say so based on the amount of slides of ladies legs he had. He required his nurses and librarians to wear skirts, nylons and high heels at all times. He loves cats and all animals and supported the Humane Society and money from his will was donated to them. He was a regular to NYC and was known to frequent the Magickal Childe bookstore. He had met Sybil Leek at some time and invited her to his Covenstead. His ladies, foremost of which Phoebe, encouraged him to get initiated by her and start a Coven. In 1967 that happened and they received their charter from her. They titled the Coven of the Catta after the cat totem as I have written before and that coven continues to this day with a short hiatus of rituals from 1979, the year of the bookhouse fire through 1980 the year of his death. I wish I had arrived a few years earlier than I did to meet this intelligent, wonderful and weird man and magickian.

Dr Frederick LaMotte Santee died on 11 April 1980 aged 72 after a long battle with liver failure. His body is buried at the Old River Church just north of Wapwallopen, Pa. His gravestone says "I shall return when Spring's shadow trails."

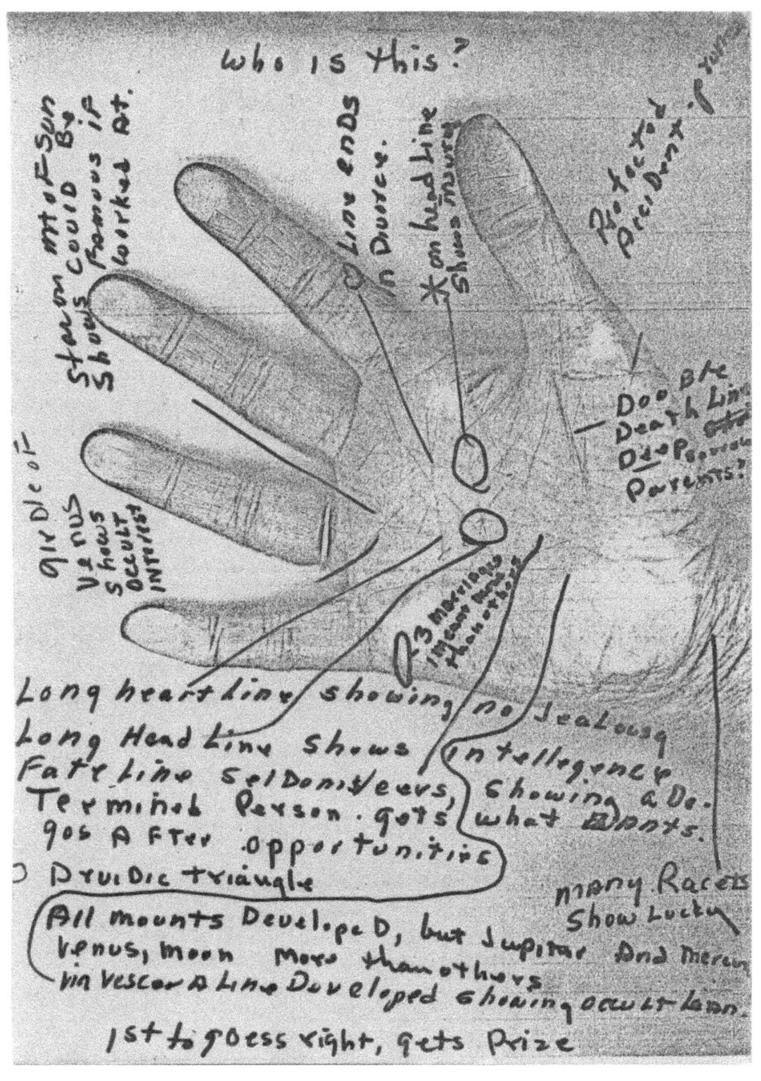

Santee Palmistry from

***The Cat's Tale* magazine**

Local scholar dies in Wapwallopen

Dr. Frederick L. Santee, 72, 5 River St., Wapwallopen, died at his home Friday at 10:35 p.m. following an extended illness.

A son of the late Dr. Charles L. and Verna Lloyd Santee, he began his practice in Wapwallopen in 1956. Prior to that, he had practiced medicine in Baltimore, where he also taught at Johns Hopkins University.

Dr. Santee was graduated from Harvard University, and Oxford University, England; Johns Hopkins Medical School, and universities in Berlin and Rome.

He was a classics scholar, who taught at Temple and Lehigh Universities.

Dr. Santee also wrote and published a number of books, the last being "The Devil's Wager."

A veteran of World War II, he served in the South Pacific.

His wife, the former Betty Addis, died in 1965.

He was the last surviving member of his immediate family.

Services will be held Tuesday at 1 p.m. from Old River Church, Wapwallopen, with the Rev. Chesley Laite, pastor of St. John's United Church of Christ, Wapwallopen, officiating. Burial will follow in the church cemetery.

The Heller Funeral Home, Nescopeck, is in charge of arrangements.

Santee Obituary

Old River Church and Graveyard

Photo by Michelle Beck

Santee Grave 2001 © GLHoke

Santee Biography Source Documents

From the Harvard Yearbook 25th Anniversary of the Class of 1924

Home address: 5078 Orville Ave., Baltimore 5, Md.

Office Address: 5200 Wright Ave., Baltimore 5, Md.

Born: Sept. 17, 1906, Wapwallopen, Pa.

Parents: Charles LaMotte Santee, Verna Caroline Lloyd

Prepared at: Central High School, Philadelphia, Pa.

Years in College: 1920-1924. Degrees: A.B. magna cum laude, 1924;

B.A. (University of Oxford), 1926; M.A. (ibid.) 1929;

M.D. (Johns Hopkins University), 1938

Married: Edith Rundle, Dec. 13, 1928, Allentown, Pa. (divorced 1942)

Betty Addis, 1942, Cumberland, Md.

Children: Ruth, March 18, 1930

(married W. J. McKnight, Feb 14, 1948).

Occupation: Physician.

Military or Naval Record: Lieutenant (Medical Corps) United States Naval Reserve, 1943-45.

His entry in the Harvard Year Book:

"I am the youngest member of the Class, probably the least successful, and possibly the only one who has never revisited Harvard. Perhaps these facts, on which my claim to uniqueness is based, are somehow interrelated. For years I kept up a correspondence, written largely in Latin, with my great teacher, the late Professor E. K. Rand. Writing Latin was the most valuable thing I got from Harvard. Many of you will, I fear, conclude that I got little else of value. My life has been beset with poverty and turmoil. It is a story of repeated attempts to root myself somewhere, of repeated failures to hold fast to my chosen career as a college teacher, in a world in which few can be taught, fewer still want to be, and a socialistic habit of thought reduces even those few to uniform patterns of empty gesture. Three lonely and studious years abroad -- the most strenuous of my life -- as a Sheldon Fellow and Fellow of the American Academy in Rome led to six years of precarious teaching at Lehigh and Vanderbilt. Surrounded constantly by a few devoted students, I did my real teaching extra-curricular, was ousted by the depression, and became first a Realsilk salesman, then a medical student. Immediately after graduation from medical school, I seized the first teaching position offered and for four years played a small part in the humanistic revival at Kenyon College. I opposed our entrance into World War II, was promptly drafted, and commissioned by the Navy in the Medical Corps. Three years of service here and in the South Pacific left me heavily in debt, since I had to support two families living in different places. By the end of the war, inflation and the needs of my dependents had advanced so far that I saw that the salary of an ordinary college professor would be inadequate. After four months of working with employment agencies, I could wait no longer. There was nothing to do but practice medicine. For low initial outlay and quick returns, I selected a government housing project on the outskirts of Baltimore. Before a year had passed, Stringfellow Barr and Scott Buchanon invited me to join them at St. John's on a salary I thought might suffice. The same year their finances collapsed and I had to buy back my old practice. Here I am in a dreary neighborhood, ministering to a demanding people, and more and more giving thought to their ills only for the sake of money I hope they will pay. I recognize that money is my only aim in life as it should have been from the start. In religion, I lean towards Anglo-Catholicism, am a member of no church. In politics, I believe in the decentralization of government and as little government as possible. I am a pre-New Deal Democrat."

From the Harvard Yearbook 50th Anniversary Class of 1924:

Frederick LaMotte Santee was born September 17, 1906, in Wapwallopen, Pennsylvania, the son of Charles LaMotte and Verna (Lloyd) Santee. He prepared at Central High School, Philadelphia, Pennsylvania, and received an A. B., magna cum laude, in 1924 at Harvard. He received a B. A. in 1926 at the University of Oxford and an M. D. in 1938 at Johns Hopkins University. His marriage in 1928 to Edith Rundle ended in divorce in 1941. In 1941, he married Betty Addis, who died in 1966. He had one child, Ruth, born in 1930 (deceased 1968), who married (1) William McKnight, (2) Juan Zaragoza, and (3) Alfred Jenanyen. There are two grandchildren. A physician, in general practice, Santee writes:

"If you don't know the poem that served as a model for these verses, you have not done a good job with your grandchildren:

How pleasant to know the good Doctor

Who writes all this horrible stuff; (1)

Some call him a scoundrel and rotter,

But a few think him pleasant enough.

His mind is abstract and fastidious,
His nose is remarkable big;
Were he only a little less hideous,
You would say he resembles a pig.

When he changes from far specs to near specs
The children are frightened and cry,
And their mothers shout, 'Hey! Don't you dare hex (2)
Poor Sam with your terrible eye!'

He has many friends, layman and clerical,
He sleeps every night with his cats,
His body is perfectly spherical,
His office girls never where flats. (3)

His office is unsanitary
With pictures of girls on the wall,
Every week he drinks gallons of sherry,
But never gets tipsy at all.

He is silent with people who talk a lot,
He won't look at women in slacks,
His favorite flavor is chocolate,
He rails at inflation and tax.

He hides in the depths of the cellar
While his patients call down through the flue,
'Come out of that cellar, you yeller,
You yeller old lazy bones, you!'

He reads, but he cannot speak, Spanish,
He still prefers women to men;
Ere the days of your pilgrimage vanish,
He hopes you will see him again.

Footnotes :

(1) Refers mainly to a newspaper column called the 'Country Doctor.'

(2) Actually he belongs to a coven of witches.

(3) A psychologist sees a relation between his fetish for high heels and his love of cats.

On rummaging through papers at the Library I also found a Master's Thesis that a visitor wrote about the Coven, containing the following bits of information I have copied verbatim:

Dr. Frederick LaMotte Santee:

Fourth generation Doctor

Grandfather in Civil War

Father graduated from Lafayette College and Jefferson Medical School in 1901, died 1963

Frederick attended Harvard at age 14 (youngest ever), graduated age 16, Oxford graduated 18, University of Berlin in 1924 for PhD, completed degree age 22, additional years in Rome, teaching positions at Harvard, Temple, Kenyon. Johns Hopkins, no tenure, one of the 100 members of the Institute of Arts and Letters

Knew German, Latin, Greek, English, Hebrew, could read Spanish, a little Sanskrit

Knew W. B. Yeats and Thomas Agee

In England initiated into the Golden Dawn and Theosophical Society

In USA Initiated into the Rosicrucian Lodge

Knew Crowley, Fortune, Regardie, Waite, and Blavatsky

Quote from the Thesis: "This interest in occult subjects seemed to culminate in his activities in the 'Coven of the Moon' in 'Little Town', where he could teach this knowledge. Although he did not care to practice ceremonial magic, he considered himself a teacher and researcher in many occult fields. He conducted experiments with a fair degree of success, but this was not his emphasis."

M.D. at Johns Hopkins in the 40's, on father's death returned to town to continue father's practice, dispensed his own medicines, office and home in same building, two nurses and four office girls, later investigated by the DEA.

Coven formed in 1963 under urging of head nurse "J".

On questioning individuals he seems to have been pushed into High Priest position to please his girls, charter for coven in 1967, although HPS should be leader actually Santee was the leader, instructed approximately 50 people during his Priesthood.

Believed he was a witch, but didn't believe in spirits because he never saw any, held a belief in a Universal Force he presumed to be God, felt that explanations of the psychic were in the individual instead of from outside forces, believed the Magick of Wicca is centered in male/female polarity, he was both social and solitary, he kept his thoughts and feelings to himself, kept his anger hidden, owned another house on mountaintop he'd retire to at times, his house/office in town being the center of activity in Wapwallopen, which was open to all as was the library also.

The Coven of the Catta Today

Over the decades there have been lots of stories told about the strange ole doctor and his coven. Some of these have taken on the style of what is called an urban legend. Some residents in the little town of Wapwallopen think he was a Satanist and his coven sacrificed cats. Reports of a supposed haunting in a house across the street from Santee's house and bookhouse brought in The Pennsylvania Paranormal Association and luckily I found out about this and gave my version of the story before it was filmed for the Animal Planet in a series called "The Haunted". The story is called "The Coven of the Cat" and you can view it on Youtube.com

The Coven of the Catta and I also have listings at Witchvox.com

Over the years various people have lived in Santee's house while the bookhouse continued to deteriorate and be vandalized. The property is now purchased by a new owner and being restored.

As I said the Coven of the Catta continues today with rituals still being held in Berwick and north of Harrisburg Pennsylvania. Here is a list of initiations after I arrived in 1981.

Image courtesy Adonis Merlin

Note – For the sake of privacy all living subjects, except for the author, are referred to only by their legal first name and/or their witch names.

From 1981-87 I (Gary Lee Hoke) was initiated into 1st degree as Shawnus, the 2nd degree as Merlin, and 3rd degree as Belarion. In 6/25/1988 Lady Phoebe Athene Nimue initiated me into the 3rd degree. She of course was initiated by Lord Merlin who was initiated by Lady Sybil. I initiated Lady Alsace Isa Brie into the 3rd degree. Alsace had been in the Coven for years beforehand. During my early years learning from Lady PAN I hand copies 3 Books of Shadows from the intact and fragmented BOSs that she had. After 9 years I turned the coven leadership over to others and continued to attend until the coven mostly fell apart. The Coven of the Catta continued with solitary witches in the Harrisburg area having occasional rituals using the format of those in the Books of Shadows and sometimes embellishing on those.

Here are the witches I have initiated. I initiated the females and the females initiated the males as per our tradition.

I initiated Iska Nuit Aradia (Patty) into her 1st and 2nd degrees. She was initiated into her 3rd degree by her husband Imago Alphanathea Satseteon (Bruce) who was initiated into all 3 degrees by his wife. They live in Harrisburg, Pennsylvania and no longer practice COC witchcraft that I know of.

I initiated Lady Alsace Isa Brie (Jeannie) into the 3rd degree 6/25/1998. She had previously been initiated into her 1st degree and 2nd degree by Lady Phoebe and Lord Merlin. She now lives in Berwick Pennsylvania. She still practices the COC rituals with me.

Pheonix Lucan (Jeff) was initiated into his 1st degree by Lady PAN 6/1990, and later into his 2nd and 3rd degrees by Silver Ravenwolf of the Black Forest Coven lineage. He now lives near Carlisle, Pennsylvania. He is also a practitioner of German Powwow. He still occasionally practices the COC lineage rituals with me.

Chiram Abii (Steve) and Levanna (Kelly) were initiated in 1987 into their 1st degrees by me and Lady PAN and later were initiated as Naxul-Rael and Lavanara-Oshun into their 2nd degrees 6/28/1988. They later initiated each other into the 3rd degrees, then left the coven and now live in Maine.

I initiated Shambleau (Debra) 8/6/1989 into her 1st degree and then initiated her into her 2nd degree as Oya 3/10/1990. She still lives in York Pennsylvania.

I initiated Augur (Jeanette) into her 1st degree 2/2/1993, then she was initiated by Iska and her husband into her 2nd degree as Nagi 2/2/2003, and I initiated her into her 3nd degree as Astarte 4/3/2004.

Scores of people started their Probationerships but few of them went further. Lady PAN initiated Dave in the Berwick area into his first degree and possibly his second. I do not know his witch names. He died of an unfortunate accident falling down the cellar stairs and breaking his neck a few years ago.

In the winter of 2008-2009 I took all my hand written Books of Shadows and typed them into Word documents. All of the rituals were already in that format. This took months to do and they are now on CD and flash drives for COC initiates. Since then the Books of Shadows have also been photographed page by page and are now in 3 PDF documents.

Three hand copied Books of Shadows

© GLHoke

Now at age 57 I live with my two black cats in the mountains along a stream near Newport Pennsylvania. I still have my original Books of Shadows compiled from Lady PANs Books of Shadows, which I cherish. I occasionally do the COC rituals with Alsace, Phoenix and Adonis Merlin. Mostly I do the main rituals alone in my inside or outside temples. I have a good relationship with a handful of mostly 3rd degree witches in the local Black Forest Tradition.

I received permission from my elder Lady Alsace Isa Brie and the only other practicing 3rd* Lady Augur Nagi Astarte that it is time to share with the Black Forest Coven lineage of Silver Ravenwolf our rituals, formulas and spells, but not the initiation rituals or information only for a Probationer in the COC. This is based on what Lady Phoebe on her death bed told Lady Alsace when asked "what about the Coven?" her answer was "it's up to you". We can keep these seeds in a jar in the cellar, or sow them on the fertile ground of deserving, respectful, and initiated BFC High Priestesses and Priests.

In February of 2010 Lady Alsace and I have initiated Adonis Merlin (Matthew) into his 1st and 2nd degrees. He is presently taking on Probationers while I continue to only work with 3rd degrees in other lineages.

As far as I know the following people are still practicing he COC system - Alsace, Pheonix,

Augur, Adonis and myself Shawnus. So as you can see the lineage of Dr. Frederick LaMotte Santee and Lady Phoebe Athene Nimue of the Coven of the Catta continues strong to this day, growing, changing and initiating those who are worthy of this honor.

Part II – Coven of the Catta Unique Ritual Practices and Spells

Introduction

I have previously written and published on Lulu.com *A History of Dr Frederick LaMotte Santee and the Coven of the Catta (*ISBN # 978-0-557-85997-9). In that book one can read the strange but true story of the doctor and the coven. To summarize, the Coven of the Catta was started in the mid 1960s by Lady Sybil Leek initiating Lord Merlin aka Dr. Frederick LaMotte Santee who then initiated Lady Phoebe. The coven continued in that form until Santee's death in 1980, and then my Priestess and I arrived in 1981 and revived and ran the coven in the little town of Wapwallopen in NE Pennsylvania until around 1990. From that point on the coven met less frequently but the rituals were celebrated in Berwick and in the Harrisburg Pennsylvania area until the present day. During that time I was also able to copy Lady Phoebe's Books of Shadows into my own copies.

In the last two years I have taken my three hand copied Books of Shadows and turned them into Word documents and put them in various files that I considered public since they appeared to be copied from other books. I also wrote biographies which I had compiled from what Phoebe told me about Santee, and what I consider secret documents for those in the initiation process. One of the public documents I titled *Coven of the Catta – Unique Ritual Practices* and another one entitled Coven of the Catta - *Teachings Blessings Spells Rites Magickes and Formulas* and these have about 58 pages of writings condensed from the 300 pages in my Books of Shadows. I have tapped the expertise of a witch friend who has read almost everything published and has a great memory to let me know what is truly unique in the coven's practices. I do know that the Books of Shadows are loosely based on Lady Sheba's *The Book of Shadows* and *The Grimoire of Lady Sheba*. Other rituals and spells are from other books published in the 1960s to 1970s. But there are many practices which are quite unique and I wish to share them here. I am not compromising anything which I would consider secret teaching which are reserved for Probationers and Initiates only.

I can see in the rituals both the hands of Lady Phoebe and Lord Merlin. I think the more traditional practices came from her and she copied a lot form the books she had read in the 1960s. I can see his hand in the parts which look and feel more like Golden Dawn material, a group he had been initiated into in England.

I am writing this book with the understanding that most of its readers will already be practicing if not initiated witches in some lineage. So I am not giving the bare elements of witchcraft rituals but only those practices which are unique.

Coven of the Catta Basics

Origins

here is the origins of the name Catta from various online dictionaries: Catta = A cat, early Irish catt, Welsh Cath, Cornish kat, Breton kaz, Gauliksh cattos; Latin catta, perhaps also catalus; English cat, German katze, etc. It is a word of doubtful origin; possibly, however, Celtic, and applied first to the wild car, then to the tame Egyptian cat introduced in the early centuries of the Christian era. The Greek katta is in later Latin cattus which means cat or cats. So Dr. Santee being a Greek and Latin classicist probably combined Katta and Cattus to make the name Catta for the Coven of the Catta.

In the Coven of the Catta the Goddess is Diana Astarte and the God is Pan Faunus. Diana is the Roman virgin Goddess of the moon and the huntress. Astarte is the Canaanite Goddess of the sky and the stars. Pan is the horned Greek God of the wilderness and sexuality and Faunus is the same in Roman mythology.

The origin of magicke and witchcraft was said to come from the Watchers, whether you think of them as "fallen angels" or as an alien race. This legend is from the apocryphal Book of Enoch. When I watch the TV movie *Stargate* I think we can see a more modern version of this legend where the gods adopted by humans were actually powerful advanced angel aliens who were both good and bad or ascendant and fallen in dualistic terms. I think in medieval times we saw these beings as angels but nowadays we see them as UFO aliens on the physical and astral planes. Between my second and third degree initiations I had my own personal experience of a female Watcher similar to Semjaza who was connected with the star Sirius-B which profoundly affected me, and her teachings flavored my magickal development. Witchcraft is magickally, psychologically and viscerally deep, which is why I use that word instead of the later revisionist politically correct New Age name Wicca even though I know that word has valid roots. It is just my personal choice and I do not care what people call our religion. My lineage is nowadays called Old School or Old Guard and I was trained in a magickal world that was neither black nor white but grey.

When I was copying from Lady Phoebe's Books of Shadows I came across this writing called *The Legend of Diana and the Nephilim*. It seems it is copied from Paul Huson's book *Mastering Witchcraft*.

Legend of Diana and the Nephilim

This is especially for those who are thinking of taking up the Path of the Goddess and for those who have not made up their minds as yet. Never the less, The Legend is beautiful and as old as Witch history can be:

In the beginning the Great Darkness, Diana, divided herself into two equal forces, night and day. The night was ruled over by Diana herself as the Moon, the day by her alter-ego and brother, Lucifer, the Sun. Diana, inasmuch as the Moon is ever pursuing the Sun across the sky, became enamored by her brother the Sun and seduced him in the shape of his pet cat. The offspring from this union was a daughter, Aradia, the archetypal avatar or patroness of all Witches.

In this Legend of Diana with it's Gnostic overtones, there are reflections of the Cabalistic tradition of NAAMAH, the seductress of the fallen Angel AZAEL. NAAMAH is synonymous with the Babylonian LILITH, and AZAEL is none other than the Babylonian SHAMASH, the Sun god in his underworld aspect as The Lord of Riches and the Artificer of Metals. In fact he is the alter ego of

Tubal Cain himself. NAAMAH's own brother AZAEL or AZAZEL, is in fact one of the modern Witch's gods.

Which brings us to the crux of the matter: AZAEL, according to the ancient magickal tradition and legend, was originally one of those beings of primordial fire, first created dwellers in the high heaven, referred to by the Christian church as messengers, or angels, and by the Greeks as daemons. AZAEL and his followers according to old lore, in defiance of their masters, elected to descend upon the Earth countless aeons ago, for the purpose of education and civilizing primitive man as he then existed.

From the ancient Book of NOAH written several hundred years before the birth of Christ is this passage: And the Angels, the children of heaven, saw and lusted after them, the daughters of men and said one to another: Come, let us choose wives from among the children of men and beget us children..., and all the others together took unto themselves wives, and each choose for himself one, and they began to be in among them and defile themselves with them, and they taught them charms and enchantments, and cutting of roots, and made them acquainted with plants . . . and AZAEL taught men to make swords, and knives, and shields and breastplates, and made known to them the metals of the earth and the art of working them. SEMJAZA taught enchantments and root cuttings, ARMAROS the resolving of enchantments, BARAQIJEL astrology, KOKABEL the constellations, EZEQEEL the knowledge of clouds, ARAQUIL the signs of the earth (husbandry), SHAMSIEL the signs of the Sun, SARIEL the course of the Moon.

According to that collection of ancient Cabalistic lore, the Zohar, Great AZAEL and his cohorts had had to assume tangible bodies in order to descend upon the Earth. Because of their revolt against higher authority and the ties with this world which they had subsequently formed, they were unable to divest themselves of these material forms and re-ascend into the heavenly spaces again. It is from these exiled beings that all true Magickal Knowledge and Power is said to be derived.

The Eight Sabats

In the Coven of the Catta we were taught the names of the 8 Sabats differently than the more modern Wiccan revision based on the Celtic names. I think our system came more from roots in the Catholic church. We were taught Candlemas instead of Imbolc, the Spring Equinox instead of Ostara, May Day or Lady Day (the day the Lady of natures comes back out of the underworld of winter, also named for a feast of the Virgin Mary) instead of Beltane, Beltane for the summer solstice instead of Midsummer or Litha (probably from Lady Sheba's books), Lammas the same as it is called today, Autumn

Equinox instead of Mabon, All Hallows instead of Samhain, and Yule the same as the winter solstice is called today too.

Leadership

The Coven had 4 main leaders, the High Priestess, High Priest, Summoner and Handmaiden. When my Priestess and I arrived in 1981 we were taught that the High Priestess ruled over the High Priest and the coven. And that was the way it was under Lady Phoebe as she taught us. But I think back when Santee was alive that the High Priest actually ruled as what others call the Magister with the High Priestess as Magistra, and that was because of his strong intellect and personality. We followed the cycle of the year where the Goddess and Priestess ruled from May Day to All Hallows and the God and Priest ruled the other half of the year. We followed the legend of Persephone's descend into the underworld which fitted that cycle. We were not taught anything about the Oak King and Holly King cycle. I always felt that there should be a balance of power but with the balance slightly tipped towards the Goddess and Priestess since we all come from the Goddess in our physical and spiritual births and rebirths.

We had a Handmaiden of the temple which we called the Vestal Virgin, a term which is too politically incorrect to use nowadays. But she was the daughter of one of the coven members and assisted the High Priestess in her role, handing objects to her when needed and just being useful and helpful. She could not be considered for a Probationership for initiation until she was 18 years of age. The temple was always considered astrally active even between rituals and thus always had an astral bubble around it. The Maiden broke into that bubble by being first into the Temple before ritual set up since she was pure. She went in and set up the altar and lit the candles and such before ritual. Then the High Priestess and High Priest went into the circle.

We also had a Summoner which traditionally went around and informed all the coven members of when a ritual was to be held. Now we have email and texting. The Summoner was the helpmate to the High Priest and assisted him in ritual. I had no such help and just did everything myself. I saw the Summoner as being similar to the Tyler in Masonry who stood at the doorway with a sword guarding the circle. Later in my participation in the coven when others were designated to do the Priestess and Priest roles I took on the role of Tyler with my sword.

Probationership

An applicant to the lineage first became a Probationer who could come to rituals, learn rituals, but had to keep it all secret. Nowadays I have heard this introductory role referred to as a Dedicant. If we or they decided to not continue, they were still bound to silence and had to return the material we had shared with them. We went through Probationers like water and my Book of Shadows is full of crossed out names of those who decided it was too much work or too scary. The Probationership lasted a year and a day, during which time they had to start a Book of Shadows and at least copy the Tenets, consecrate a bolline or working white handle knife, then from that cut and consecrate a wand and besom, consecrate an athame and cup, make an altar cloth from a very specific pattern, and make their red cingulum. The sword was usually temple owned.

In our Coven we chose a new witch name for each degree we achieved, thus all third degrees had three names. The sigils for our degrees are an upright triangle for first, upright pentagram for second, and hexagram for third. I used a Crowley unicursal hexagram design.

Initiation

Initiations in the Coven of the Catta are pretty much like most Gardnerian lineages. We definitely require a year and a day between Probationership and the first degree, and that time is usual between all the degrees. There are ordeals for all the degrees and these are of course to test perfect love and perfect trust. The ordeals are pretty much standard fare and since these are published in books in the last few years I have decided to craft the ordeals for a particular postulant based on what I have learned about them and their particular fears.

There are two ideas of what initiation means. The most common idea is that it is a seal of approval stamped onto the initiate that they have achieved a certain level. Another view, which I hold from experience, is that initiation is an opening of a doorway towards achieving that degree. So an initiate of a degree is given the keys to their new status, but there is a road perilous to walk until that goal is reached.

The degree symbols are a little different from those used in Gardnerian or other lineages today though in Lady Phoebe's BOSs she listed both sets of symbols but I was taught this one. The sigil for the first degree was the upright triangle, not the downward one. The sigil for the second degree was the upright pentagram, not the obverse. And the sigil for the third degree was the hexagram. Since I am also into the Thelemic system my hexagram was unicursal, drawn with one continuous stroke of the pen.

I will reflect that I have seen many witches get what is called "second degree fever" where they all of a sudden feel powerful and start acting in an arrogant way. I think since my Priestess and I basically took on the roles of Priestess and Priest from the beginning before we were even initiated that we avoided that. Our coven almost fell apart from some other seconds who just wanted to grab all the power. I will also admit that it took us awhile to get out third degrees because our teacher did not particularly like the ritual we had to write and perform for our initiation since it contained Thelemic and Stellar magickes init. It took a few years in our growth process and that of our teacher to be able to ge through this time when one's Jungian shadow and the Lurker at the Threshold in the Abyss between the Sephiroth so to speak have great influence. It was a great test of all of our wills and maturity to continue on.

Tools of a Witch

Listed here are the tools required of a Probationer witch before Initiation into the 1st degree of the Lineage of the Coven of the Catta. I am listing the basics and not giving any specific information on the sigils or consecration of these tools, though most of it can be found in the standard Solomaic grimoires. Unless you were a blacksmith, all the tools of the craft were hand made except the athame, cup and sword. The length and height of tools were based on measurements based on one's own body dimensions.

Basic Altar Setup © GLHoke

Bolline – white handled knife

The first instrument for a witch to find or make is their working knife or bolline with the handle painted white. This is a sharp edged knife with which many of your later tools can be manufactured. There are specific sigils to be engraved on the blade. I found an old butcher's knife at a flea market which had been ground down over the years to a useful size of about a foot long which I could use to chop and cut and engrave wood with. Of course the bolline is also traditionally used to cut herbs with. If I needed a blade that is more specific to some task, like my Boy Scout knife, then I would transfer the energy of the bolline to it by rubbing the edge of one onto the other.

Athame

Buy or make an athame, which must be a double sided symmetrical blade, and it is best if it isn't sharp because it isn't used for cutting anything and could take an eye out during rituals! Paint the handle black if practical. There are specific sigils to engrave or paint on it. After the consecration three days before the full moon, which I will not give here, carry out this dedication task. Plunge your athame into the ground in a place most secret to the hilt with one plunge, leaving out a yell fro your soul. If it hits a rock and doesn't go in the whole way, take it out, wipe it off, and try again next full moon. Leave it there three days and three nights before the full moon. Concentrate on the Universal Force (akasha) and see it entering the blade. Charge the athame to bring a piece of Life Force whenever there is need. On the full moon night pull the athame from the ground. Cleanse it with a cloth and be careful to not touch the blade with your hand as the blade is never touched except for initiations. Too bad about those rust stains and scratches on that nice shiny new blade bought at the new age store! Put a drop of blood on the athame. Put the athame away into a special bag or box. The athame can be recharged by putting it outside or on a windowsill in the light of the full moon.

Wand

Cut your wand in the spring or summer between Spring Equinox and Lammas when the sap is up in the tree. Use your bolline if possible, or transfer the energy of it to a saw. Oak or rowan is best, but any tree which produces fruit (nuts or fruit) is fine. The length of the wand is the distance between your fingertips and the inside of your elbows. Carve all the bark off of it. Drill a small hole in the positive end. During the consecration put a drop of blood into this hole on a piece of cotton and seal with green wax. There are specific sigils to carve or paint on it and then the wand is oiled or stained or painted to your liking. I wrote the sigils on mine in red ink and then used redwood stain on the whole length. Note that the sigils we were given I have never seen in any books and they seem to be a combination of runes. I was able to cut my besom and wand from the same piece of a high oak tree branch right before a thunderstorm. That way no tree was killed in the process. I still encourage witches that if they are cutting a young tree to cut it above one of the lower branches so it can continue to heal and grow.

Besom

Like the wand, the besom is also cut in the spring or summer between Spring Equinox and Lammas when the sap is up in the tree. Use your bolline if possible, or transfer the energy of it to a saw. Oak or rowan is best, but any tree which produces fruit (nuts or fruit) is fine. Make an offering to the tree of coppers (pennies) or any other offering you may come up with and a drop of your blood. Leave the wood outside for at least a month for it to cure. The length of the besom is the distance from the ground up to your shoulder, though some like one head height. Carve the bottom into a blunt point. Remove the bark from the top and carve into a simple phallic shape. You could also remove all the bark and use the entire length for your carvings. I used the ogum alphabet to carve my magickal name on the top. The besom can be decorated as you will with bells and symbols and whatever you want but I kept mine fairly simple. You can also consecrate with oil. Many covens nowadays buy or make a broom for their besom but ours was more of a tall walking stick. Lady Phoebe told me the phallic end of the besom could be hidden inside broom material and hidden that way in the house. The besom also represented the witch when they were not present. In the Coven of the Catta temple behind the altar were besoms of those who had passed on.

Altar cloth

I am not going to give any details of this object since it is for initiates. But it is made from a piece of white cloth that is the length from your fingertips to your armpit. It is sewn using red yarn with a certain numbers of stitches around each side with a magickal design in the middle. Your witch name is also sewn into it. With this altar cloth you can set up an altar everywhere since it is portable.

Book of Shadows

Purchase or make a blank book. We just bought large blank artist books with black covers at an arts and crafts store. Later I took silver paint and made my own sigils and names on the front outside cover. I had to buy fountain ink pens to copy with and when the ink cylinder was done I was instructed to bury it in the ground. If a pen became unusable I did the same.

On the first inside page of the book we would draw the witches pentagram and then put our witch name in the middle of it and prick our finger to put a drop of our blood on it. Copy into this BOS the Tenets, then all rituals and spells as they are given to you. Record all the dates of your

Probationership and Degrees. You can also record when and how you made each of your witch tools and any psychic or visionary experienced you had during this process and during any rituals. It is a book in which you can copy the past and write your own unique spells and such.

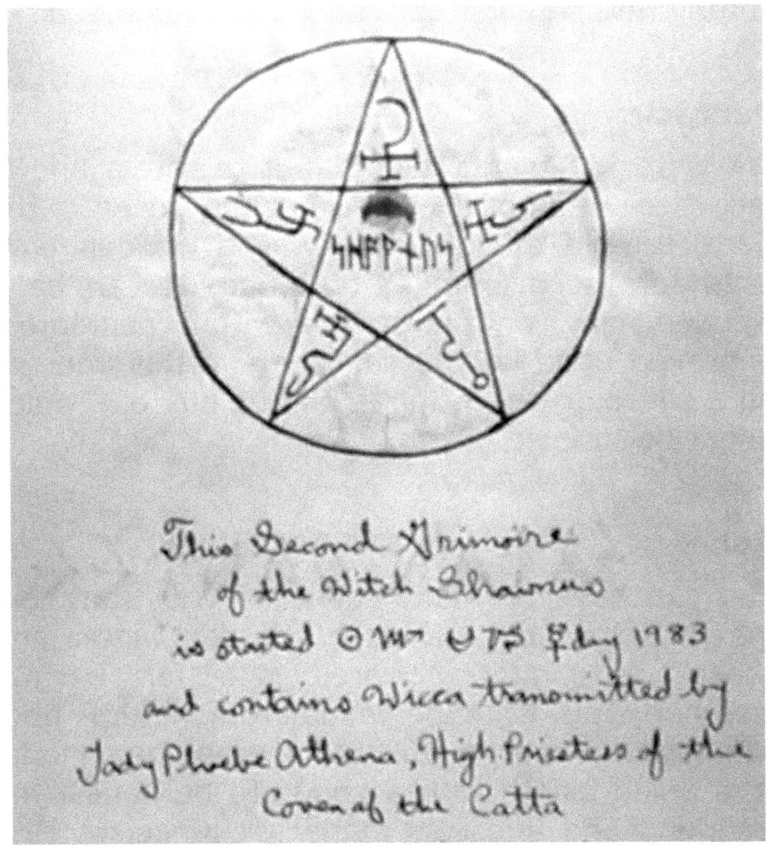

This Second Grimoire
of the Witch Shamans
is started [illegible] 1983
and contains Wicca transmitted by
Lady Phoebe Athena, High Priestess of the
Coven of the Catta

Book of Shadows Dedication Page © GLHoke

Cup

Buy a silver, pewter or ceramic cup of your liking. Catholic supply shops actually have simple classic cups better than those at New Age stores. The cup can be engraved with your name and the name of the coven since it can also be a coven owned item like the sword. It is consecrated with certain herbs at a stream during the full moon.

Pentacle

We were not taught much abut this item and in fact there was not a pentacle at the Coven of the Catta temple though there was a wooden bowl used for the sacrament of bread. It can be a wooden, clay, or metal circle with a pentagram engraved upon it. You can engrave this yourself on a silver or pewter plate or just buy one which might be simpler.

Robe

You can have as many robes as you want, but may want to have a dark one for winter and green or summer colored one for warmer weather. This is to be made from natural fiber like cotton or wool or silk. It has to be handmade. It is ankle length with a hood. To be honest my girlfriend and Priestess made me make my first robe by hand using her sewing machine. The rest of my robes were made by other ladies or ordered online.

Bell

The bell is used during ritual at the evocation of the Watchtowers and at All Hallows to call the dead. You can engrave it with your magickal name and the name of your Coven.

Cingulum

I am told the use of cingulums in the Coven of the Catta are unique to our lineage. Other covens call these cords of rank. We only have three, a red one for the first degree, silver for the second and black for the third degree. We were required to hand make our first red cingulum and mine was woven from 4 skeins of red cotton yard using a knitting knobby top used for spool knitting which I bought at a craft store. The four strings got woven into a tube shape into which you could insert your hair, fingernails, blood, herbs etc as it was woven. It was at first to be about a foot longer than your height to account for the knots to be tied and it ended up being the same length as your height. Knots were tied on one end measuring your height, then the circumference of head, chest, waist and hips, then a final female loop at the other end. They were tied around the waist with a specific knot which made an ankh form. The red cingulum was also considered one's umbilical cord to the Goddess and could be used to connect to the earth or moon. In one's initiation ritual it was connected to the altar. For the silver and black cord we were allowed to buy them ready made at either a drapery store or Catholic supply store.

The cingulum can be secretly worn underneath your clothes even when not in ritual. It could be wrapped around one's head to meditate. Power could be "blown" into an object through this cord. Stand facing East and twirl your cingulum deosil several times, forming a purple cone of power which will form a white circle of protection for you. Sit with cingulum laid in a circle around you, visualizing the star or your initiation degree on your forehead. It could also be used in binding spells and as a cable tow in initiations.

Witches Mark

This is a silver piece of jewelry which makes an unbroken circle, like a ring or bracelet. Engrave inside it your magickal name. This was used to contact the energies of your lineage and of your Coven. I considered it to be a sign of my marriage to the Goddess. I have read in modern witchcraft this ring is given to a witch at their second degree, and in light of this marriage it makes sense to me.

Witches Ladder

This is a necklace or rosary of 40 beads of stones of your astral sign or choice. The number 40 is considered a perfect number in Kabala and in Witchcraft. It is 5 X 8 for the pentagram and the eight fold Wheel of the Year which equals 40 and added when added together makes 13 for the number of lunar cycles in a year. Another meaning of those number is because of the 8 fold kiss where you kiss 5 areas on the body which are actually 8 places because we kiss the two breasts, knees and feet. This is considered the "perfect working couple". In other traditions a witches ladder is a cord with 9 knots but we were never taught that.

Censor

Buy a swinging censor or make one from a brass or copper cup from a flea market and chain from the hardware store.

Scourge

It can be bought or made from leather and wood and can have the sigil of scourging upon it, which is like a $ with the cross piece at an angle. The scourge was used only in degree initiations and was used lightly over the robe, seldom directly on the skin. Of course what you use it for in your private rituals is up to you. This is also unique because in other Old Guard rituals, the scourge is used at the beginning of each ritual via the women scourging the men and then men scourging the women. And it was also used in raising the cone of power where a witch would act as the conduit of the energy in the center, her/his working partner would perform the scourging while the other participants would funnel the energy to the person acting as the conduit to channel the energy. But like I said in the Coven of the Catta it was only used in initiations.

Tattoo

Lady Phoebe had a woad blue tattoo on her upper thigh of a crescent moon with three stars above to represent her three degrees. I copied that tattoo on my left thigh when I reached my third. We were never told to get this tattoo, but it has become a tradition amongst the third degrees.

All ritual items can be recharged by putting on a windowsill or out in nature in the light of the waxing to full moon.

Basic Full Moon Ritual

And now a big decision for me. Decades ago I shared a copy of the basic Coven of the Catta full moon ritual upon which all the other rituals are based. I did this to assist an up and coming author whose works have blossomed into many titles and editions and I do not regret that decision. The original copy had my name, the name of the coven and a copyright on it. No one until recently has abused that and tried to publish it as their own. I have been to rituals with other covens and found them using this ritual, which is fine with me because they seem to really appreciate and cherish it. But recently I learned of a book published in 2005 which had parts of our rituals in it but not mentioning the COC origin. Apparently a copy of the ritual got in the hands of a magickian in NY and he shared it with the author despite the copyright. My first knee jerk reaction is to publish the basic ritual so it is copyrighted in a book so others cannot claim it as their own. But then I have to remember that in the vows of my first degree I promised to not share the secrets of the coven except with initiated witches. So I have decided to NOT publish that ritual. I do share some parts in this book but not enough that you could put the entire ritual together, so I think I am remaining within my vows. Here are the unique rituals and spells which I do feel comfortable sharing with other witches.

Unique Ritual Practices

From this point for the sake of simplicity I am going to refer to the High Priestess as HPS and the High Priest as HPT.

The Coven of the Catta temple has the floor painted with 3 circles starting from the inside circle 9 feet in diameter painted in light blue, then a middle 11 foot circle painted dark, and finally a 13 foot outside circle painted silver. These directions are from Lady Phoebe's Books of Shadows and I have never seen them anywhere else. Some research shows that these are the colors of the Priestess path in the Tarot which goes from Tiphareth to Kether on the QBL Tree and perhaps Dr Santee having training from the Golden Dawn added this scheme.

The altar is in the north bridging between the earth and the north pole star.

Over the doorway at the entrance of the Temple was a sign with the words "Know Thyself" in Latin. I am sure Dr Santee added this since he was a Latin and Greek classicist.

Before ritual the HPS and HPT were to take a bath in a special herbal formula to cleanse their auras. We were told to fast or at least not eat meat for a day and we were told to meditate before the ritual.

As written before, the Handmaiden is first into the circle to light the candles and prepare the altar.

She is the one who is pure enough to break through the astral egg that is always active in the temple even when the circles are not yet cast. That was one teaching I found unique that the energy of the temple was always accessible to the coveners even between rituals. They could leave their besoms in there to represent themselves and could light their astral candles at home to tap into the energy since these were lit from the main Crown of Success candle during the one flame ritual (more of this later).

When casting or dissolving a magickal circle we go ESWN and then salute the East again, thus completing the circle, like a period at the end of a sentence. When casting a circle the HPS or HPT makes the first circle scraped on the ground ESWNE with the sword, leaving a doorway shape for the coven to enter later. The second circle is cast with the athame held at chest height. The third circle is a censor swung EWEWEW X 3 then NSNSNS X 3 (or the other way around) then swung around over one's head deosil X 3 thus making a sphere with 4 quarters.

The Coveners stand in a line outside the circle until it is cast. After the salt water is consecrated by the HPT a pentagram is made on their foreheads with the O Lord Adonai blessing. After they enter the circle the door left open when the circle was cast is now closed left to right with the. If anyone really needs to leave the circle it is opened with the sword right to left then closed left to right again.

The watchtowers are set up by giving 4 witches the symbols of the quarters (E incense, S candle, W water, N salt), and when that quarter is evoked then kneel down and hold that symbol up. The watchtowers are called by first making a pentagram with the athame by first kissing it, then pointing to the top point, kiss, then top to bottom right, kiss, then bottom right to top left, kiss, then top left to top right, kiss, then top right to bottom left, kiss, then bottom left to top. This is considered the pentagram for evoking the element fire and we did not use any other of the various pentagrams that can be traced for the other elements nor did we use a banishing form at the end. Then the archangel is evoked into that watchtower. The bell was rung thrice after the evocation.

After the watchtowers the Greek names of the God and Goddess IO EVOHE are chanted three times, dragged out to EEE-OOO-AAA-VOO-AIEEE with a Blessed Be at the end.

Next in the ritual the HPT stands in the East with arms and athame pointed up and chants Ex Oriente Lux (Out of the East comes Light) to invoke the solar God and to bring this energy down into the circle. This would be the male equivalent to the HPS calling down the moon. I can only assume Santee added this invocation.

The normal Charge of the God is used by the HPT to invoke the Horned God. At the end during the chanting of IO PAN this Priest adds the LUX body signs of the Golden Dawn and OTO.

As the HPT helped the HPS call down the Moon Goddess into her she would start out in the position of the Virgin or Venus with hands across her yoni, and then manifests the Goddess of the Moon with arms held up in a crescent moon form. These are the Puella and Mulier mudras in the NOX signs of the OTO.

Then the Coveners file past and honor the HPS as Goddess with a kiss on her right cheek, forehead, and left cheek, then bowing or curtsying giving the sun-at-midnight salute (see below).

The sign of the God is the right handed "peace sign" with index and middle finger in a V like horns with the other fingers folded to the palm. The sign of the Goddess is the sun-at-midnight with thumb and little finger extended with the other fingers folded to the palm, not the index and little finger extended as in the hard rock cornu salute. These signs are used to salute the Goddess and God statues on the altar when entering the temple, and to salute the HPS and HPT when they have invoked their deity. When a witch of equal or inferior degree greets a witch of equal or higher degree, they give the God or Goddess salute. First one kisses one's fisted hand in that sign, then makes the sign while the men bow and women curtsey. To not do so is a sign of disrespect and ignorance. I am told the sun-at-midnight salute is used in some modern covens but the God peace salute is unique to our coven.

The Orange Crown of Success candle was always lit first on the altar, and all other candles lit from it. Due to its color it could represent the Sun at times but mostly the Full Moon. Each covener had an astral candle of the color of their astrological sign. This was lit from the orange Crown of Success candle for the One Flame ritual where everyone held their candles together and rededicated themselves to the coven. These were then placed on the floor behind them to make an astral flame of their aura behind them. They were left in the temple between rituals, the temple always being astrally active as mentioned before, so each Covener could tap into the bubble of magickal energy of the Temple and Coven when needed. Or these candles could be taken home to one's own altar for the same purpose.

In an old York Pennsylvania coven that two of our coveners previously belonged to they had a black Mother Candle which was in a permanent place in the temple with black wax dripped down all around it. This represented the primeval Dark Mother Goddess. This practice has recently been adopted by this Priest. I think the black and orange candles balance each other out for the sun and moon and bright and dark phases of the moon.

To prepare for the sacrament we do the Seven Holy Breaths in which the HPT or HPS stands and faces ESWN raising their arm up and down as coveners breath in and out cleansing the elements in them of air for mind, fire for heart, water for emotions, and earth for body.

The cone of power is raised by joining hands and swinging them back then up to the Hebrew God name Yod He Vau He (father, mother, son, daughter, ending in a loud Yod with the arms up when the energy built up was blasted out to its destination. We would go around the circle asking for requests for healing and magickal work to be done. At the end the more psychic witches would tell what they saw happening. Then at the end we did the same to heal the earth, something which I added which also helps ground the energy raised.

High Court was adjourned if a covener has a disagreement with another covener and resolution could be in the following ways:

1) That person is to talk to the HPS and HPT.

2) Person is to talk to the other person in the presence of the HPT and HPS.

3) If that doesn't work then High Court is held where the 2 people sit in the midst of the coven and the HPT and HPS enthroned. The decision is made by them. The offender has to make a knee bend to the other. That person then decides on a funny penance, and all is made in balance with joy again.

This Priest's specific practices

Many of the circle set up parts can be done either by the HPS and HPT or even by the Summoner, Maiden, or a helper Covener. At the COC we of course had a Temple set up. Nowadays one's temple or circle is in a room in your house. It is my practice that is the circle is held at the house of the HPT then he should cast the circles and if at the HPS house she should do it, since one's own magickal space is already set up

I also like practices I see today where the circle is cast deosil ESWNE and then dissolved widdershins. But i noticed the dissolving of the circle starts in the East. Shouldn't it start in the North, where the casting of the circle ended? I first saw this in Black Forest rituals and have adopted it for my personal rituals. The casting would be puling down the elements from above to the temple as air, fire, water then earth. The dissolving would be earth, water, fire then air as the Watchers returned to their stellar realms.

I like to add the Archangel Metatron at the zenith and Sandalphon at the nadir of the circle cast with the normal watchtower angels of Raphael, Michael, Gabriel and Uriel at ESWN.

Any witches, Priestesses and Priests who read this may feel free to adopt any of these practices if it is their Will.

Magickal Methods and Spells

Everything in this section is typed from my hand copied Books of Shadows, which I copied from Lady Phoebe Athena Nimue's Books of Shadows in the early to mid 1980s. Some of these spells and formulas may have been copied from the libraries extensive occult book collection published in the 1970s and in those cases the copyrights of course belongs to the original authors. Of course many of the spells and writings came from books by Sybil Leek and Lady Sheba and those I have deleted. I have had the remaining spells painstakingly reviewed by a witch who has read a lot of books and has a great memory and he advises that these seem unique to the Coven of the Catta. But if anyone recognizes one of these spells or rites as being from an older book please notify the author and I will delete them from this work.

A Self Blessing

Make a cross and circle around you touching your forehead, sex, right shoulder, left shoulder, then make a horizontal circle clapping your hands together in front of you and then behind you then again in front, saying:

In the Name (touch forehead) of the Goddess (touch sex) Diana (right shoulder) Astarte (left shoulder) protect me in all things (front to back to back to front circle).

Psychic Methods in Witchcraft

Make a triangle with the tips of your index fingers and thumbs with the rest of your fingers woven together beneath (like here's the church here's the steeple hand positions). Two triangles will be formed, the larger one is oneself and the smaller upper one the Goddess. Entranced, look into the triangle of the Goddess for guidance.

Hold objects up to your third eye or hold in your hands and let your intuition lead to visualizations which will reveal the vibrations in the object.

To contact the energy of your Coven circle touch your witch's mark (ring, bracelet, necklace) and travel there or visualize the Coven's cone of energy shooting towards you.

Power from the Air is gotten by cleansing oneself as before a ritual, then in nature "see" the energies swirling as silver streaks around you, harmonized through breathing. Grab hold of these lines of force and dance, wind them around you, pull, love, embrace, use the energy for your purpose, then ground it.

Charge an object by holding it between the solar plexus of a man and a woman embracing. Charge and harmonize yourself by standing back against or embracing a tree, feeling the upward balanced energy.

A Tree Spell – by Lady Phoebe

Trees are a good source of radiant vitality on a very low frequency scale, and this can be drawn upon under favorable conditions. A very useful application of it is for relief and even cure of many backache conditions. This process is as follows. Select a suitable tree. It must be a strong upright tree, free from distortions or malformation and of good size. Any tree but yew will do. And if it is on a forest it will be better than on the grounds of your house. Make friends with the tree by talking to it, touching it, and thinking into it. circle it nine times, either touching it with the fingertips or with your staff. Take up your final position north, and lean back against the tree firmly as if in the arms of a friend (which it is). Reach your hands behind you, touching the tree as if you were holding its hands, and say or think slowly and deeply:

O tree, strong tree, kind tree, take thou this weakness of my back. give me thy strength instead, that i may be upright as thyself between the heavens (look up) and the earth beneath (look down) secure from storm and blessed in every branch. So mote it be.

After this has been repeated a number of times until a sense of rapport is felt, relax quietly against the tree and slowly let it work for perhaps ten minutes or so. breath slowly and deeply, thinking of nothing except peace and tranquility. After a little, there should be a pulling out feeling in the back which varies with individuals. When it is felt that the treatment is over, break contact gently, thank the nature spirits for their help, pay the tree by sticking a pin into the bark, and take a small piece of the bark for a pocket link to carry with you.

This process can be repeated with a number of trees so that one's linkage with such natural sources of healing are thereby increased. The healing process with trees is often slow, and instant cures are not very likely. An original method of using trees for healing is similar to the foregoing, except that the diseased part of the body is rubbed with the ribbon of rag which is then tied or fixed to the trees with an iron nail. This forms the necessary link. Two famous such trees are the Virgin Mary's tree at Matarea and the tree near the Nile where Moses was said to have been found in the bulrushes. The Glastonbury thorn was once used in such a way. Try to work this spell with the feet bare so as to establish good earth contact.

Ritual to attune the spirit, mind and body to the growth energies of Spring

Use one white beeswax candle. Pile greens and flowers and coins around it. Light it every midnight for 15 minutes until done, chanting:

As Spring lengthens, so will my scope widen, my soul deepen, and my body strengthen. I will understand what I see, and know what I don't see exists. Thus will it always be.

Burn and bury all when done.

Ritual to enchant a well or spring for holy water

On the night of the full moon stand before the spring, saying:

Blessed be, water of life. Blessed be by the Patroness of us all.

Toss silver coin into the water.

With this silver I give to you a gift of the earth and the moon of silver to keep you clear as you come from the earth, as She shines on thee.

Toss lily of the valley and woodruff and hyssop into the water.

I toss these herbs to you O water of life, the lily for sweetness, the woodruff for purifying thee, and the hyssop for protection. For me ye shall smell sweet, be pure and protected, and clear as the silver moon, as I work with thee, for I work with the Lady of the Moon.

Stand with feet on dry ground and hands in water, saying:

O water of life, from now to the day I die, I will keep thee sweet and pure and protected. I ask only of thee that when I have need of thee, that thou will be there. In the name of the Patroness of us all, Be Blessed as I am blessed as I enter two elements at one time, the most magical place on this planet. Blessed Be.

Water is prepared at this time for use in ritual. Keep it fresh and in a dark place. During the waxing moon it can be place in Her light. Refresh the spring every so often with the herbs.

To banish a person from the Coven

Take all objects belonging to the person and burn them outside, then burn candle over it, cover all ashes with dirt, cover hole with a white cross.

Ritual to consecrate water goblet

Cleanse with salt water. Fill with pure water and the herbs hyssop, lily of the valley, woodruff, sage, artemisia, wormwood and yarrow. Chant ritual for consecrating and enchanting a spring to the Goddess (as above). Charge cup with water and herbs in the light of the full moon.

Coven healing ritual

The Priestess heals a man and the Priest heals a woman. The genders in this ritual are given for a female healing a male.

Sit or lay him in the center of circle in a comfortable position with limbs uncrossed. Surround him with 13 candles of his astral color.

Coven sits outside circle of candles facing in. Priestess lights candles deosil from the orange crown of success candle on the altar, doing and saying at each numbered candle:

Candle # 1

Hold candle above ill one saying:

I do charge you in the name of our Lady of Healing and of her power to heal to put aright the body and give release from pain.

Candle # 2

Blessed Be.

Candle # 3

Hold candle before his face saying:

Now as you gaze steadily at the simple flame see only its light.

Candle # 4

All those about this circle shall concentrate steadily on your healing.

Candle # 5

All ye who site about this circle of candles.

Candle # 6

Hear me and do as I say."

Candle # 7

Look closely at the one who is ill, and picture clearly the pure life force flowing from all who sit here strong and powerful into the afflicted body, there to remain and strengthen until healing is done.

Candles # 8-13

Priestess lights the rest of the candles as all sit and concentrate until the ill one says

The rite of healing is finished

He stands up.

Maiden puts candles back out from patient in order deosil. Each covener takes candle home to continue to work at the same time each day for 15 minutes until the candles are burned down. Bury wax and matches together near Covenstead.

Healing a drastic case

Take 13 musk incense sticks and put all together in a cauldron of sand. Coven all sit around ill one holding hands. Light incense sticks one by one chanting:

Hyah, Hyah, Hyah (sounds like AmerIndian chanting)

All meditate to burn out the illness and replace it with healing musk.

Healing with oil

Take olive oil and put in 3 drops of healing oil, rose oil and sandalwood oil each. Coven sits around 13 candles as before with ill one comfortable in the center. Priestess or Priest of opposite sex as patient starts to oil down ill one at place of affliction. Each covener takes turns doing the same concentrating on feeling illness being drawn out, then at the end all are massaging him together, pleading the ill one's cause and thanking the Lady for healing. (this Priest would suggest since this is a drawing out ritual to then use a paper towel to wipe the oil off the covener's hands and then burn it so it doesn't stick to them). Each take a picture of the ill person home, oil up a candle of his astral color from the center to both ends, then at the same time all burn their candle in front of that picture. It is suggested to keep the ill one busy with little daily rituals to distract him from depression and pain as the healing works. The ill one after this ritual may need to use the bathroom quickly afterwards as the toxins leave his body, so be prepared for this.

Recipe for witch's ink

Find a pokeberry bush, stand in front of it, and explain what you need the berries for, see right berries, cut and thank, then plant one see by the bush. Grind to juice in mortar and pestle and strain the seeds out. Add 3 berries of deadly nightshade ground up. Add 3 drops of your blood. Store in dark bottles. Set in full moonlight. Use quill to write with. Throw away old ink when you make new. Note this does not make a black or purple ink but rather a brown color. I have seen other recipes where there are better formulas in which the mixture is allowed to ferment which will produce purple ink that lasts longer. Also I learned these berries are poisonous so keep away from children and pets.

Rituals for banishing psychic attack

Draw outward to inward widdershins a spiral in a doorway in the air to protect room from evil interruption as a devil trap.

Use incense of hyssop, sandalwood, frankincense and cat straw as a burning fume to scatter around circle.

Cut onion in half with bolline, banish with athame, bless with wand, use athame to cut pentagram on it, place over doorway, change once a week.

Lead water - cleanse and bless water and salt with athame, mix, cleanse pieces of lead and charge with pentagram, pass lead through fire, charge in names of God and Goddess, put lead in salt water and place under eastern window for one week of waxing moon, use new brush to paint lead water on walls, around room, Priest paint upper line, Priestess paints middle line, Handmaiden paints lower line.

Stand west with feet splayed out in a duck foot V and hands in outward pointed triangle upside down V in prayer, chant loudly and slowly *Mathra!* over and over.

When being attacked use the very powerful words *Ana Ana Temptu. Eine Eine Temptu* which evokes the Goddess Hannah.

Word talisman to fend off psychic attack: Write person's name thrice on one side of paper without pen ever leaving paper in one flowing script. Then write person's name backwards as a mirror image on the other side the same. Burn and say protective chant, then flush it away.

To tell where psychic attack is coming from hang your athame by your cingulum or a string and as it spins around and stops the blade points at what direction the evil is coming from.

Full Moon (Banishing) Ritual

In my BOS this is called a full moon ritual, but it seems more a ritual to banish evil spirits and bring good spirits in through the Priestess at the Full Moon.

Priestess spreads sulfur around circle, leaving a doorway, saying:

Evil, remain at bay, only capture and enslavement can result from your invasion of our temple.

Coven enters, holding their athames outwards of the circle saying:

Spirits of Evil, you may not cross this line.

Spirits of Good, come to us.

Priestess closes sulfur circle with branch of evergreen, then hands Maiden herbs to make circle within of cleansing and protective herbs.

Priest says:

All Spirits above and below us hear now of my warning, if any be evil or malicious you will be trapped by our magicke and made to work. If you are not afraid, stay. If you are afraid, go now and forever hold your peace.

Coven says:

Evil Spirits above us or below us, go or forever hold your peace.

Priestess lights candle, goes to the East and kneels saying:

Spirits of the East, see this guiding light, come with the rising sun and moon to visit us.

Priest lights candle, goes to the South and kneels saying:

Spirits of the South, see this guiding light, and come from the fiery heat of the sun to visit us.

Priestess lights candle, goes to the West and kneels saying:

Spirits of the West, see this guiding light, and do not follow the sun and moon, but come and visit us.

Priest lights candle, goes to North kneeling and says:

Spirits of the North, see this guiding light, and come from the cold to its warmth to visit us.

Coven joins hands together, all dance deosil, then stop and point athames at Priestess,

Priestess in Goddess position with athame held up saying the Call of Nine (not unique to the COC):

Gracious goddess, holy and divine,

Answer to the call of Nine.

One, I stand before they throne.

Two, I invoke thee alone.

Three, I hold aloft my blade.

Four, descend, as the spirit is made.

Five, lend thy power to give it life.

Six, thy power, into my knife!

Seven, on earth, in sky and shining sea

O Gracious Goddess, be with me.

Eight, come now, thy call is made!

Nine, give thy powers unto my blade!

At the end of rite transform all power from your athames into bowl of holy water, bottle and distribute to covenors.

Coven says:

Thank you for your help friends and Goddess and when the moon is full, come again. Go now and rest content as we pray you to help us in the coming month. Good night and blessed be.

Priestess brushes circle away.

Love charm

Gather three strings of the color of sun, moon and earth. Tie together and place in small earthenware jar for six days. Add juice of jasmine flower. Press all together to get an inky fluid. Take white cloth that has been steeped in barley water and dried. With this ink and cloth write this magickal square in first hour of the day.

H B B N N

R H B N R

B R H B N

N B H R B

Place square between two flat stones in your room for two days. On second eve say loudly to it the name(s) of the persons you wish to enchant into love together. Repeat for three days, and the result will be accomplished.

Poppet for Money

Gather white cloth and make into poppet, wool for hair, green cloth to wrap it, marigold, cinquefoil, loadstone, dollar bill and change, and green candles. Sew poppet at full moon to new moon to symbolize your need. Sew green $ signs into palms of poppet. Sew symbol of Taurus onto groin for man or back to back crescent moons for female. Night before new moon fill poppet and money up to sky and say:

Goddess of plenty, sweet helper of the needy. This is (name) whose resources have wanes always leaving sorrow and great need.

Hold up poppet left hand and $ right hand, saying:

This is the substance that has been drained from (name). Lady of the Moon, as thy disk waxes in the heavens, let good fortune was for (name) supplying him/her with the money he/she so sorely needs.

Store money and poppet in green cloth. Keep until fulfilled, then thank, and dismantle.

Poppet for Love

Similar to the above ritual. Use white cloth, red thread, and red wrapping cloth, violet leaves, nightshade, magnet, and object from desired lover.

Goddess of Love and beauty, sweet helper of the needy, this is (name) whose heart I wish to capture as he/she has captured mine, and I am lonely and without him/her.

Hold up poppet left hand and magnet right hand.

As the Moon waxes, bring him/her to me.

Green candle money ritual

Take a green candle and cut a cross on it. circle the candle deosil and chant:

Green of money, come to me,

Rest in my hand hastily.

As you burn, O candle green,

Let money now be seen.

Candle made of wax and wick,

Do my spell, and do it quick!

So mote it be. So mote it be. So mote it be!

Light candle quickly now.

Mirror spell

To fend off energies of an enemy or undesirable.

Surround image of this person you wish to bind with mirrors or foil.

Mirroring (name) hold thy image tightly bound

As we dance the circle round and round

Let (name)'s magicke turn back to self

As we turn to you requesting help

As our word, so mote it be!

Repeat thrice while coven circles. Coven stops and directs will to shield person with mirrors to keep his magicke in.

Candle ritual for healing

Use candle color of ill one's astral color. Put a pin in the candle to symbolize their illness. Pray to the Goddess. Burn candle until pin drops out to symbolize their illness leaving them.

Spell for harmony

Take a green candle and on it carve the vertical opposing crescents (like a U on top and an upside down U beneath), a circle, and three concentric four sided diamond shapes. Anoint with oil and cense with incense promoting harmony. Sing your spell to the Goddess over the lit candle the put the candle out and chant:

Even though thy flame be out

Harmony will spread about

This home and land and everyone

Will feel thy love, O Triple One.

Egg spell to control a person

Take an egg and empty it completely. Put into it the sweaty clothes, fingernails, feces, hair, etc of the person to be spelled. Seal with wax. Put red string into the end of it. Baptize the egg in the person's name. Store egg in a dark place. Every so often take the egg out and tumble it in your hands saying the Words of Commandment: *Allah Ayeh Allah Shimballah!* Release your wish to control such and such. Re-store egg in dark place.

Group working with a red yarn wheel

This may be in some books but I have never seen this particular method used in a coven except in ours.

Cut red yarn cords about 6 feet long, one for each covener. Tie a knot at one end of all of them to hold that end together. Coveners form a circle each taking an end of the string holding it taught so the hub of the wheel is held above the ground and never touching it. Coveners make silent wishes and tie a knot into their thread until they reach near the center, never letting any part of the wheel touch the ground. The Maiden or Priestess then goes to the center and picks the wheel up by the hub and hangs it up in the temple to do its magicke. Next Sabat the wheeled cords are burned.

Spell for protection

This spell was given to Lady Phoebe in visitation by the discarnate spirit of Lord Merlin through Lady Alsace.

Stand facing East and twirl your cingulum deosil several times, forming a purple cone of power which will form a white circle of protection for you.

Protection of a House

Use small mirrors or silver Christmas balls. Draw pentagram, arrow with point up and 9 lines across the shaft and a hexagram on the backs of the mirrors or on a parchment to put into the Christmas balls. This will reflect all evil back to those outside.

To make a magicke mirror for scrying

Take a small round mirror. Draw pentagram, arrow with point up and 9 lines across the shaft and a hexagram on the back. set into a box painted black. Cover with black velvet. Never let light hit it. Place two candles around the box, then you can open the box and scry.

Harvest apple

Take an apple and make a hole in it and put a beeswax candle into it. Put leaves and berries around it. burn every night, giving thanks.

Methods to protect from psychic attack

Onion slices - place around house inside, change weekly.

Iron water – put some iron into water inside house to set up electromagnetic field you can charge.

Burnt salt – 3 times a day for 3 days burn some salt over charcoal, then wait 3 days, then repeat 3 X 3 until evil gone.

Draw pentagram over your head with athame.

Witch's cross (see previous witch self blessing).

Burn sandalwood – burns lots of it, cense walls and floor and ceiling heavily in all rooms of a house.

Wear salt in tissue in a bag, change weekly.

Sit with cingulum laid in a circle around you, visualizing the star or your initiation degree on your forehead.

For lovers to depart

Take 2 pieces of string, one slightly larger than the other. Baptize each string in the names of the lovers you wish to part. Tie 3 knots tight with those 2 strings, saying:

(Name) and (name) tight you are together though you will not stay. Each day i will break his/her spell on you. and to me he/she will stray. As my work so mote it be.

Each day in the hour of Venus loosen the knots a bit until parted over 3 days and visualize him/her coming to you. use the string of your desired lover for love spell.

To make an iron water magickal wall of protection

Obtain some water from a natural source, not out of a tap, at full moon. Place a piece of iron in the water and set in moon light (its shelf life is until the next full moon). Take a brush and paint a line around the walls of the room or temple. The crone, priestess, and maiden can draw these at three levels around the room.

To find which direction evil is coming from

Hold your athame out with both hands going ESWNE until you feel a direction the athame is vibrating. This is the direction evil is coming from. Take a two sided mirror, wash thrice in chamomile water or fluid condenser, hold it up to that direction, and see yourself protected from that evil.

Preparing the land for a magickal herb garden

Mark off the land to be used with sticks and strings. Determine and mark the four directions with stones. At twilight build small fires at four directions or use votive candles. Start at north, plant and light candle, moving deosil until circle complete. Stand center of garden facing north with athame lifted skywards, saying

I (name) call upon the powers of the north to bless and protect this garden.

Repeat at all four quarters. Turn north and trace pentagram in the dirt with your athame. Turn south and trace downward triangle with sun sigils above and below and moon sigils right and left in the soil with athame. Sit quietly and meditate. You can also go and cut a branch of the nearest sacred tree and leave a branch in the middle of the garden as payment to the spirits. The next morning at sunrise search the ground for symbols left by the spirits like feathers and symbols in the grass etc. Then pour one quart of apple cider vinegar from an earthenware vessel around the garden deosil. Let the ground soak it up and leave. The garden is now blessed.

Candlelight service

In the middle of any Sabat or Esbat, or during a private ritual, a candle can be lit by a covener for their wish, blessed by the HPT, and placed on the altar by the HPS. Any negativity can be written in pencil on paper and burned during the ritual. And wishes can be put in pencil on paper and burned thusly also to send them through fire to fulfillment.

Addendums

Poems:

Invocation from Lord Merlin to Lady Phoebe

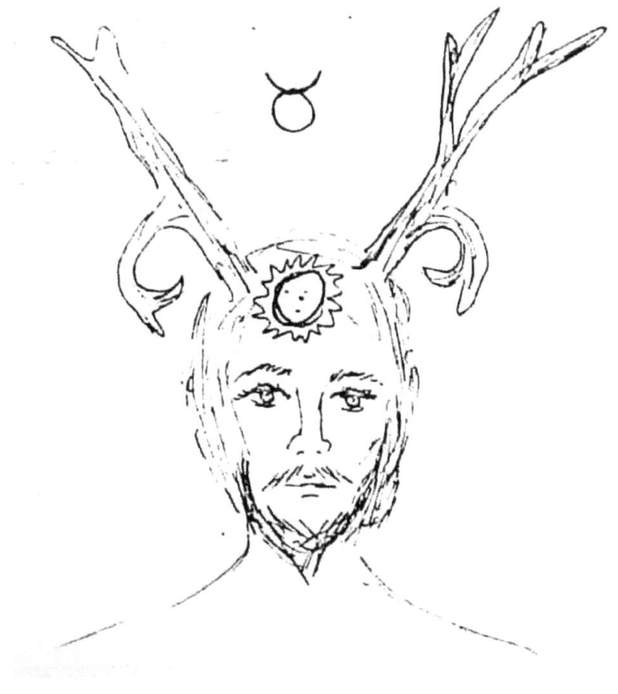

I AM HE

Like a god I can wipe away the clouds form the sky if you want it blue. I will pull down the stars to light your room at night if you want me to. Tomorrow i will level off the mountains and drain the sea to make room for the palaces I have planned for you. Like a wall I stand between you and anything that might threaten your joy and peace. The kings and captains of the earth will wait outside to adore you on your new throne. While I live you will is law. The magic power I draw from you makes me invincible. There is nothing I cannot learn or do, no problem I cannot solve if you let me do it in your name and for your sake. The world has no existence for ma apart from you. it has no meaning but what you give it. You are the cause and the purpose of all my deeds. If you leave me, my world will fall apart. Unless some other SHE comes quickly to the rescue, I shall die. To renew my strength, I have only to look upon you or touch you, and I go forth conquering in your name. What is it in you that revives and inspired me? I call it beauty. But this is only you creating and expressing yourself. For you are SHE.

Invocation from Lady Phoebe to Lord Merlin

I AM SHE

I walk with you in the twilight that falls like fairy dust around us. My silvery rove and midnight blue cape swings in the gentle wind of the gods. No matter my gait, no mater whether I be slim or obese or my beauty be the beauty of 18 or 80, for I will always walk straight and tall, my slim legs twinkling under the cobweb silk of my robe. I am always willowy as the figure of SHE and my beauty if forever. I willingly allow you to be my wall between danger and myself. I willingly allow you to worship at my shrine. You have earned that privilege of adoring at my feet for I am SHE. You can do naught without me. The veiled Isis can be unveiled to you only if I am at your side. But I need you in order to be SHE. Without you I will be nothing as you are without me. with your strength and my beauty we will face and conquer the twilight of our world without fear, for you are HE.

From an Unknown Bard at the Covenstead

Hymn to the Sun

I awoke this morning ere
    the light's dawning birth,
And saw the earth awaiting
    that light and warmth,
Like a lover awaiting her love,
    Expectant . . . Hesitant . . .
Like it will never happen,
    yet glorying in the
        sweetness of expectancy.

The mists hover and hang in the pines,
    threads,
As the threads of fate and time
    Hang in the balance for lovers.
Will the lovers meet?
    Will their love be fulfilled?

It is yet a waking love, of small things,
    The greatness and fertility
        is yet to be.

As the earth waits, expecting its love,
My phallic pen makes love to the virgin paper,
Spilling it's ink-sperm, on and over,
Violating the purity of it,
yet fulfilling it's purpose,
giving it being,
breeding a bastardy of verse.

As I like the paper, and the earth,
Await the awakening of my lover,
To meet, love, conceive,
and give birth to a new day.

Now the earth quickens,
as her Sun-Lover approaches,
The birds, hymn singers,
begin the nuptial music.
The folds of her body,
The hills and valleys covered by green pubic-grass,
are damp with the love juices of dew.

The Earth-Mother sits and awaits
The first thrust of the Sun-Father,
tremblingly,
With the thoughts of this wanted love,
hesitantly,
Awaiting her virginity to be violated.

Night maid, Luna
Lesbian lover of the night,
Steals away, fades from sight,
by father-sun's brightness.
Now quietly, the night creatures,
attendants of the lesbian Luna,
hide from the brilliance
of the earth's true lover.

The hymn of the birds grow louder.
His maleness draws closer yet.
The earth quakes.

The day creatures,
after the night of quivering fearful sleep,
begin the preparation to welcome
the sun lover.

Sun-Lover begins his ritual of
golden caresses and kisses
On cold expectant Earth . . .

Now slowly, the men and women,
Children of previous lovings,
begin to stir.

The lamps of the houses,
nestled in the folds of the mother,
gleam in feeble paean to the
sun, father, lover.

The earth mother is now warm, now hot,
Ready for the first thrust
of her lover's golden lance of light.
Ready to shiver in delightful orgasm
of creation.

But, yet he hesitates.

She is not brought to a final peak,
Ready for the first mighty lunge.

The earth awaits yet awhile,
        Knowing her lover is near,
        her body bursting with energy,
        covered with love dew.

As I await,
I hear the stirrings and preparations
        Of my lover for the dawn's loving,
        in feeble imitation of nature's
        labor of creation.

I hear the footsteps of my love
        on the stair,
As the orange footsteps of the earth's lover are
        seen over the green-blue horizon.

I rejoice in expectation as does the earth.
My lover is close at hand
As I begin the ritual of caresses and kisses
        that prelude the act of creation.

As the sun kisses and caresses the earth,
We both, Sun and I,
Glory in the perfection of the body spread before
        us . . .

Now she is ready for my maleness,
As the earth is,
Awaiting the golden thrust of the sun,
To bring the orgasm of creation.

Now as the sun-lover first plunges
his golden light into the earth's folds,
I meet with my lover's body, risen,
Risen from the floor to meet mine.

More rods of light penetrate,
and violate the virgin earth,
As the serious business of creation
is now underway.
The earth joys in the
first throes of orgasm,
As my lover's body trembles as well.

The earth is now fulfilled.

Her purpose of creation is come about
As a new day is birthed.

Light's sperm is spattered
all over the earth,
As new ideas and beings are born,
Some legitimate,
Some brilliant,
Some bastards.

We are now in the softness and warmth
of a new day,
As we reflect on the wonder of creation,
And already anticipate,
because we know that

This wondrous loving will occur,
Again
Again
And again
Forever . . . .

Hymn to Diana

How shall I, The Poet, sing the praises of Winter?
What virtues are there to extol?
Are ice, sleet, bitter cold,
and naked trees joyous things?

The only emotion that winter brings to mind is hope.
While walking through the eldritch beauty
of a winter landscape,
I shiver and huddle,
chilled by the iciness in my heart.
I am warmed only by the hope
that you will bring the Spring of Love,
again, to an ice-bound soul.

Memories of warmth,
Of summer's love,
Walking through meadows of pine forests,
are but torments, not comforts.

Come again to me, Goddess of Love,
Let me return, at least briefly,
            in a dream if need be,
To your summer warmth.

I long to run, naked, beneath the Sun,
            and feel the kiss of thy breath.
Comfort comes now,
            With the knowledge,
The death of winter, the hag, will soon come,
            and again we will be together,
                        My Love . . . . . .

Ritual Texts from the old Grimoires compared to those in the Coven of the Catta Books of Shadows

A comparison of passages from the *Grinoirium Verum* and the *Grand Grimoire* from Idries Shah's *The Secret Lore of Magic* compared to passages from rituals from the *Books of Shadows* of the Coven of the Catta.

From the Grand Grimoire:

O Lord Adonai, who hast formed me, Thy unworthy servant, in thine image, from plain earth: bless and sanctify this work, for the cleansing of my soul and body, and may no deceit or stupidity be her. O Most Powerful God! Through whose power the people were able to walk through the Red Sea from Egypt; give me this grace, purified and cleansed by this water, pure in Thy Presence!

From the Grimoirium Verum:

Lord God Adonay, who has formed man out of nothing to Thine own image and likeness, and me also, unworthy sinner as I am, deign, I pray Thee, to bless and sanctify this water, that it may be healthful to my body and soul, that all delusion may depart from me. O Lord God, Almighty and Ineffable, who didst lead forth thy people from the land of Egypt, and didst cause them to pass dry-shod over the Red Sea. Grant that I may be cleansed by this water from all my sins, and may appear innocent before thee. Amen.

From the Books of Shadows of the Coven of the Catta:

Priest hold up cup of holy water to the gods saying:

O Lord Adonai, who has formed me from plain earth in thine image, bless and sanctify this work for the cleansing of the body and soul. Let no deceit or stupidity dwell herein, O most powerful God. Give me this grace, purified and cleansed by water and by salt.

Priest makes fire invoking pentagram on his forehead and then on the coveners saying:

Be thou cleansed, regenerate, and purified, so the spirits will neither harm thee nor abide in thee.

From the Grand Grimoire:

May all devils flee, and particularly those who are inimical to this operation! When we enter herein we call with humility that God the Almighty entering this Circle will cast down diving pleasure and prosperity and joy and charity and greeting.

May the Angels of Peace help and defend this Circle: may discord disappear from it!

Help and magnify us, O Lord. Thy Most Holy Name bless our meeting and our speech. O Lord our God, bless our entry into this Circle, for Thou art blessed for Ever and Ever! Amen.

From the Books of Shadows of the Coven of the Catta:

Priest/ess makes deosil circle with sword on ground saying:

May all evils flee, and particularly those who are inimical to this operation which we enter herein. We call with humility that our Gods be with us to cast down divine pleasure and charity, prosperity and greetings.

Priest/ess makes second circle with athame at breast level saying:

May the keepers of peace help and defend this circle. May discord, discontent and disorder disappear from it.

Priest/ess makes third circle at head level swinging censor of incense east west three times then north south three times then deosil in a circle three times saying:

Help and magnify us. Bless our Sabat and our speech. Bless our entry into thy sacred circle.

So as you can see someone in the Coven of the Catta, most likely Dr Santee, used and adapted phrases from these old grimoires into their rituals.

An analysis of the Eko Eko Azarak Chant

Shawnus Merlin Belarion 3rd* HPT © 2009

Here is the original version of the Eko chant copied from the Books of Shadows of the Coven of the Catta, which is the same as that published in many books of rituals:

EKO EKO AZARAK
EKO EKO ZOMELAK
EKO EKO ARADIA
EKO EKO KERNUNNOS
EKO EKO DIANA
EKO EKO FAUNUS
BEZABI LOKI BACHABABA
LAMOCH CAHI ACHABABA
KORELLOS CAHI ACHABABA
LAMOCH LAMOCH BACHAROU
CARBAHAJI SABALYOS BARYLOS
LAZOS ATHAME CALYOLAS
SAMAHAC ET FAMYOLAS
HARRAHYA!

For decades I have been chanting *EKO EKO AZARAK, EKO EKO ZOMELAK* with the rest of you. These names of the Goddess and God precede the better known names of Aradia & Kernunnos, Diana & Faunus within the litany, names more familiar to us in the traditions of Wicca. So who are these deities and what are their country, culture and time period of origin? What are their forms? What archetypes do they represent? For many years these questions have haunted me. I have meditated upon them, analyzed them according to letter and number, and compared them to other gods. I have scryed their spirits in ritual at the New Moon. And I have set up a section within the All Hallows rite for these Old Gods to show themselves with the company of the dead that we call at that time. These are the Old Ones of the coven, according to the list of names we chant each Sabat. And that chant, according to witchcraft scholars, is from the Basque people in the Pyrenees mountains between France and Spain, a hotbed of hold-outs from the religions of Paganism and various Gnostic and Manichean heresies. So maybe the names are from their pantheon. To me the names sound like a combination of the languages I would describe as Sumerian or Gnostic though I am no expert in such things. Below is my analysis thru English Kabala of the letter/archetypes within these names:

A and Z are the Great Old Ones;

Azarak is the Goddess name,

Zomelak is the God's name.

A = Ah = Air/breath/life/spirit/sophia/shekinah

Z = Za =
Fire/life/energy/stellar/electricity/magnetic

A Z A R A K

6 letters = hexagram of the sun

Gematria = 1 8 1 9 1 2 = 22

A = aleph = air

AZ+ZA = Man into space +
the stellar into man

AR = fire wheel

RA = the Sun

K = kundalini

AZA = Z as the stellar flanked by
the double aleph A A , and thus,
the Egyptian Double-Wanded-
One Hrumachis

RAK = Ra + Ka = the Sun +
the Soul or double

Z O M E L E K

7 letters = the number of Venus

Gematria = 8 6 4 5 3 1 2 = 11

Z = the buzz of space, or semen enlivened

ZOM = zoom/acceleration

O = ayin = zero void space

OM = Aummmng

ME = mem = water

EL = god as the feminine spirit

LA = the feminine as Babalon

and the Moon

A = aleph

AK = airy male kundala fire serpent

Melek (Hebrew) = King of Tiphareth

Melekim = Angels of the Sun

AZARAK / ZOMELAK

13 letters = the number of the moons in a year

A + Z = the whirling Swastika

This old Basque version was shared by a friend:

EHO EHO AZARO
EHO EHO ZAMARIAC
BAHE GABE LASHA BACHERA
GARALLAZ!
LANAC LANAC BACHERAZ
KHOPORA-GEY SABELAZ
BALLYJOAZ!
LAJHAZ ETA KHOPORAZ
SEMIAC ETA FAMILIAZ
HURRAHYA!

Hard and Soft Witchcraft and Magickes

Shawnus Merlin Belarion 3rd* HPT

I am writing this article thinking about my decision to build a temple in the cellar directly under my first floor temple, and my desire, need and magickal intuitiveness to use a lot of iron. My cellar is below the water level when my fickle stream rises, and is often wet. I have my sump pump and a generator to keep it dry when the power goes off. I have always been fascinated by good ole American made metal tools that last forever, after the rust is removed. All of my garden tools are old and were originally owned by my grandfather or my dad. I have also acquired some of them over the years at yard sales and flea markets. I recently acquired a lot of old metal chisels and other tools that feel much the same as holding a Tibetan Phurba in my hands, and some old iron horseshoes aka lunar crescents. So since the center of the earth is molten iron, and I have to fight the water and earth to keep my cellar intact, I feel that making a magickal witch circle of metal tools is appropriate. Since it is below ground I need to make sure the nature spirits are not offended, but the incursive water spirits may take a step back. I love the Naga water spirits, but sometimes you need a metal dam to survive their uncontrolled desire to drown all the earth in water. I am trying to buy a large iron cauldron for down there to fill with black aquarium sand to stick iron tools into as a talisman of the power of iron, much like a Palo cauldron is used. I will use my metal athame, phurba, cup, pantacle (meaning a ritual plate not necessarily a pentagram), chains and other tools to establish this deep iron earth circle. There are "hard" and "soft" methods in witchcraft and magicke. And in contrast the next time I am out back doing a ritual by my tree stump altar, I will practice a softer witchcraft using non-metallic tools.

One of the oldest teachings of Witchcraft is that metal implements are harmful to the nature spirits and should not be used in rituals. But from the Middle Ages on witches and magickians have used metal athames and swords in their rites. The old shamanic path of witchcraft worked magicke before the use of metals was widespread, going back to the stone age and wood age. Later copper, brass and bronze were smelted for use for ornament and weapons. Silver and gold were used for ornament and tender. Even later iron and steel were made for even more efficient tools for farming and war.

I can see how the Goddess oriented religions were offended and even defeated by the warrior God oriented later religions whose kings and priests wielded such weapons of metal. I can see how the nature spirits of the trees cut down by bronze and iron axes and of the earth plowed by iron blades felt scared and withdrew into the remaining wild forests. And i can see how the natural shamans felt their pain and fear, the same as the pain and fear the pagan peasant population felt with wave after wave of foreign invaders and tribal wars.

Metal implements are the products of the male blacksmith, to be used by warriors and farmers. Wooden, fabric, plant (herbs), wood and stone implements are the products of female artisans to be used by healers and craftswomen. These are the traditional roles from 100 years ago, but of course nowadays there are female metal workers and male fabric workers.

I have practiced Witchcraft in various forms for the last 30 years. I have also practiced Tibetan Buddhist, Shaivite Tantras, Himalayan shamanic Phurba and Naga pujas, and AmerIndian shamanic paths intertwining all these paths and systems. I have blessed and used a metal vajra, phurba, athame, sword, chalice, pantacle and talismans. I have blessed and used a wooden wand, besom, pantacles and talismans, and crystal and stone wands and pentacles. But I can intuitively feel when metal is not the implement of choice in some rites and rituals, especially when working outside in the woods. I think these two "hard" and "soft" witchcrafts and magickes can both be used today, with respect for both paths, and with the mixing of these paths in modern civilization. This is similar to the hard and soft methods used in various martial arts.

There are of course the two systems of magicke and witchcraft regarding the casting of the circle. In magicke the circle is cast to protect those inside, and the use of metal implements works for that. In the witch circle out in nature the circle is an invitation to the nature spirits to come in to join us, and the use of natural implements is best for that, to "not scare or intimidate" the faeries, dryads, nyads and gnomes (though the latter, being the original miners of metals, are not offended). Ultimately tools are just an adjunct to moving energy through your hands and feet from the earth and sky and tools are used to accelerate those energies.

There are witches who live in the woods and mountains, and those who live in cites and suburbs. And there are witches who live in one world yet travel to do magicke in the other world. When I do a ritual inside in my temple in my house and home I will use both man made metal implements and nature made tools. But when I am out back across the stream at my outside tree stump altar decorated with wood and feathers and stone, I feel I should not use metal tools there since if feels too hard. I feel I need to be softer out with the nature spirits. After all, what is there to fear but their tempting illusions to leave this modern world and become a human animal spirit with them?

So maybe you can see my point here – there are hard and soft witch ways and magickal ways of working with both the old native spirits of the earth and the new spirits of our modern age of steel and electronics. And I have not even touched on the subject of electrical and internet magickes and witchcrafts, a subject for another article. My advice is to listen to the gods and spirits of the place where you wish to set up your circle. Listen to what the spirits say are the proper and comfortable ways for you to work with them and for them to be friendly and helpful and in their sacred space with you. Always discern the gods and spirits before you engage them, and never threaten or harass them since that method which was born of the schizophrenic psychology of the Middle Ages is where modern religious fundamentalism and Satanism came from. We do not need to go back to that threatening method of working from the premise of the dualism of angels and demons, unless we are working with those systems. Modern witchcraft can work with both hands. The God/ess loves you and you should love and respect and honor the God/ess with a handshake, not a weapon. But sometimes a good iron phurba or athame works best to bend the elements to one's will. Or to put it mundanely, packing a gun usually makes a handshake good enough.

Country and City Witches

Shawnus Merlin Belarion 3rd* HPT

Gary Lee Hoke © 2009

Thorn Nightwind 3rd* HPT © 2009

I see a lot of witches buying their witch tools at Wiccan and New Age internet stores nowadays. There are definitely a lot of wonderful fancy products available for sure. It is a temptation for both country and city witches.

I wish witches would make their own instruments as best they can, or buy objects at local flea markets and yard sales to turn into their witch tools. In my tradition one's tools are gathered and dedicated over a year and a day, so you can take your time to shop around. Sure I could sit down and surf the internet and buy them all in an hour or so, and I have bought lots of stuff on the internet myself, but what kind of witchcraft is that? It is more credit card magicke than real work. Don't grab your tools, but call them. Put out the call to the gods to bring you what you need, then patiently shop around locally and see what the gods throw into your lap.

I found my athame on Halloween in a friend's barn in his grandfather's tool box. It was a hand forged blade which had never been sharpened, and I wonder what it was made for and how it had lain unused for so many years. The gods gave me that athame. I found my bolline at a flea market in the form of an old butcher's knife which had been sharpened down very far with use, and all I had to do was engrave it and pain the handle white. I found my cup at the local Catholic shop. I braided my first cingulum out of red cotton yarn using an instrument you can get at a craft store. The other cingulums I bought at a window dressing store in the form of drapery cords. I bought cloth at a fabric store and sewed the sigils on it myself. I was even forced by my Priestess girlfriend to buy a pattern for a robe and sew it on her machine! I cut my own besom and wand from a branch of an oak tree in the back yard. I didn't buy some fancy BOS from an internet dealer for hundreds of dollars, but bought blank art books at an artist store and painted the covers myself. I found my cauldron at a local antique mall for $20 instead of shopping online for cauldrons with pentagrams cast onto them which were expensive plus shipping costs.

We also need to own the karma of what we buy. If we need a wood product, we need to be the one to cut that tree or branch and offer thanks. If we want a bone handled knife then we need to own the karma of the killing of that animal or at least the harvesting of its bone. Find stones out in the woods and streams to put on your altar rather than buying expensive lapidary turned stones. Strain your back, skin your knuckles and break your nails. The gods will show you what you need to find.

Of course we can't all make all that we need, but there is a witch out there somewhere nearby who is a kitchen witch, seamstress witch, blacksmith witch, wood worker witch or herbalist witch. I always remember a Probationer in my old Coven who took a piece of steel and used a grinding wheel and made her own athame blade. Now that is hard core! Even though they aren't witches, there are crafts people out there who can be outsourced to make what we need, no questions asked. Support your local talented witches and crafts persons! But if you live in a big city, then you may have to go to your local store or shop on the internet, but always choose the closest vendors you can. It is all about the local economy. It is the same with fresh food in the summer - don't buy it in the grocery stores, but go to the local farm markets if possible.

Regarding oils and powders and incenses - figure out the ingredients of the formulas sold online, figure out what plants they use, then find substitutes in herbs grown here in America. Find a witch herbalist and get them to figure it out. We don't need to buy cleansing herbs from Africa or the Middle East or Europe. Just find out what the AmerIndians used that grows here. Instead of frankincense, burn South American copal.

My witch friend Thorn wrote the following, which does not contradict what I have written, but gives a viewpoint of a country witch who has moved to the suburb of the city:

"I think Witchcraft and the way it is practiced must be modified individually so you can practice based on your own surrounding conditions. This tends to be called: "creating your own synthesis of magicke". We create this "magicke" subjectively based on our own understandings and environment... no more and no less. Any cunning or clever witch needs to be able to look around the area in which they live and become cognizant of what the Goddess has given them to work with because energy and nature is in all things. Not only must we see the beauty and power within a grove of trees, we must also see beauty and power in something so mundane as dining room furniture. You can find nature and energy in the cities and towns and you can find nature and energy, well -- in nature."

"No matter how much we try to cut down forests and turn them into parking lots and shopping plazas, nature is a consistent energy and still exists by implementing the same amount of pressure and force it always has. Over time, if we leave what we built on top of Nature; nature will return it back to a "natural" state."

"A very wise woman I love and respect taught me the following passage from one of her Vedanta classes she attended: "God does not move". The "God Energy" does not move no matter what we put in its place. There is nothing that is not of God, therefore "God does not move!" We know the essence of God is within and without everyone one of us and everything, so no matter how many times we move things, crush things, build things: It is all of God, you can't "move" God because God is everything. We are the embodiment of the Divine Creator/Creatrix. If this is the case, no matter where we are at and what surrounding we must work in, the "magicke" is there. The only limit to power is the limits we place on ourselves."

"As a witch, regardless if we live in a city/town or out in the country, we all adhere to the part of any ritual known as "preparation of the meeting place" so that we can create sacred space. Even when outdoors, we find ourselves moving objects from one place to another in order to create sacred space. It can be as simple as moving a tree stump to make an altar in the North, or making a circle or stones or a sacred fire circle – we are creating sacred space! We do the same thing inside too – we move our altars, bring in stones, etc. The Chinese even have a sacred art on a subject I think is very familiar with what us witches do… we call it creating sacred space and they call it Feng Shui!"

"Nothing dings my cauldron more than hearing: "Well, we must practice sky clad because our clothes inhibit the power directed ... okay, maybe some truth to this is certain and being in circle naked is more natural, but if you "believe" energy and power can be pushed through a temple wall -- or even pushed through a dense forest, well then by golly it has to be able to pass through our clothes without harming or stopping it."

"My other 2 cent opinion is if you take a witch from the country and put them in a city, do they know how to adapt their magic to the energy that is present in that particular space and in that particular time? Also, when you take a witch from the city and put them out in the country, do THEY also know how to adapt to that particular energy at that particular time?"

As the author of this book I have been a witch in both city, suburb and now thankfully out in the woods. I can tell you I have dragged along large rocks, pieces of wood, plants and such from the woods to ground myself when I was in the city.

And I have brought my PC and internet connection out to the country to shop online when needed. But the longer I am in the country the more I realize the resources out here for what I need to work witchcraft. I can even buy my herbs from the local Amish!

Final Thoughts

I hope this book has been of interest to those of you who already practice witchcraft in all its varied forms. Most lineages trace back to Gerald Gardner and Alex Sanders and especially to Doreen Valiente. Ours traces back to Sybil Leek and there are few in this country who can say that. There has always been the question about whether Dame Sybil ever had her own Book of Shadows and I have never heard anyone say yea or nay. If she did have one then honoring her vows she did not publish it, and as you know she was a proliferate writer with many books published. If there is such a book I would assume one of her relatives has it, or maybe it is so tucked away as to be lost. The main rituals of the Coven of the Catta are from one main ritual which I assume Lady Phoebe wrote with Lord Merlin aka Dr. Santee. Lady Phoebe copied many teachings and spells from the books which were published in the 1960-1970s, and I have tried to keep all that is obvious out of this small book and just published what appears to be original and unique. As I said before, if anyone recognizes anything from any old books whether in or out of print please write the author and this will be corrected.

Blessed Be

www.ingramcontent.com/pod-product-compliance
Ingram Content Group UK Ltd.
Pitfield, Milton Keynes, MK11 3LW, UK
UKHW020127250726
13967UKWH00002B/525

9 780557 953448